THREE ESSAYS

THOMAS MANN

THREE
ESSAYS

Translated
from the German by H. T. Lowe-Porter

NEW YORK · ALFRED · A · KNOPF

1929

ORIGINALLY PUBLISHED AS
Friedrich und Die Grosse Koalition
IN
REDE UND ANTWORT
AND AS
Goethe und Tolstoi and *Okkulte Erlebnisse*
IN
BEMÜHUNGEN

834
M31π
87892
Mar.1974

CONTENTS

I

GOETHE AND TOLSTOY

GOETHE AND TOLSTOY

At the beginning of our century a man was still living in Weimar, Julius Stötzer by name and schoolmaster by calling, who, as a sixteen-year-old student, had dwelt under the same roof with Dr. Eckermann and only a few steps away from Goethe's door. Young Stötzer and a schoolmate and fellow-lodger would now and again, with beating hearts, catch gleams and glimpses of the hallowed form as the old man sat by his window. But the lads were possessed by a desire to see him for once close at hand and get a good look at him. They applied to his famulus, their house-mate, and implored him by some means or other to procure them this boon. Eckermann was a kindly soul. One summer day he let the boys in by the back gate to the garden of the illustrious house; and there, hugely confused, they stood and waited for Goethe; who, to their consternation, did actually appear. He was strolling about the garden in a light-coloured house-coat — very probably the famous flannel dressing-gown we wot of — and catching sight of the lads went up to them. There he stood, wafting odours of eau-de-Cologne, with his hands, of course, on his back, and his abdomen to the fore; with that air of a city father beneath which, so we are told, he hid his self-consciousness — and asked the youths their

3

names and what they wanted. Probably all in one breath; which indeed, if it thus happened, so added to the austere effect that they could scarcely get out an answer. However, they stammered something; whereupon the old man bade them be diligent in their tasks — which they were free to interpret as meaning that they would do better to be at them and not stand gaping here — and went his way.

So much for that — it happened in the year 1828. — Thirty-three years afterwards, one day about one o'clock Stötzer — now an experienced and devoted master in the secondary schools — was about to take the second class of the session when a seminary pupil stuck his head in at the door and announced that a stranger wanted to see Herr Stötzer. And without more ado the stranger entered at his heels: a man considerably younger than the schoolmaster, with a thinnish beard, prominent cheek-bones, and small grey eyes, with furrows between the heavy brows. He neglected to introduce or otherwise account for himself; but simply and straightway asked what lessons there were this afternoon, and on hearing that there was first history and then language, professed himself well pleased. He said that he had been visiting schools in southern Germany, France, and England; and sought an acquaintance with those of northern Germany as well. He spoke like a German. You would take him for a schoolmaster, from the comments he made, his well-informed, intelligent questions, and the way he kept putting things down in his notebook. He stopped for the whole of the lesson-hour. The children wrote a theme, an exercise on some subject in

4

their copy-books; and the stranger said he was greatly interested in these compositions — might he take them away with him? " Dear me," Stötzer thought, " that *is* naïve." Who was to reimburse the children for their copy-books? After all, Weimar was a poor city. . . . He said as much, in politer phrases. But the stranger replied that that might be managed, and went out. Stötzer sent a message to the Director, telling him of the unusual occurrence. And the adjective he used was the correct one — though it was only much later that he understood how correct it had been. For at the moment and on the spot it could not mean much to him, when the stranger came back, with a bundle of writing-paper under his arm, and gave his name to Stötzer and the Director: Count Tolstoy, from Russia. But Schoolmaster Stötzer lived to a ripe old age, and consequently had plenty of time to hear about the gentleman whose acquaintance he had thus made.

This man, then, who lived in Weimar from 1812 to 1905, and whose life was otherwise no doubt uneventful enough, might boast of having enjoyed one extraordinary privilege: the personal acquaintance of both Goethe and Tolstoy, the two great men whose names form the subject of this essay. Yes, Tolstoy was in Weimar! When he was thirty-three years old — for he was born in the year that saw young Stötzer's interview with Goethe — Count Leo Nikolaevich came to Germany from Brussels (where he had in the first place met Proudhon and been convinced by him that *la propriété* is *le vol*, and in the second place had written the

5

story called *Polikuschka*) and visited the city of Goethe. As a distinguished stranger and guest of the Russian Embassy he was admitted to the house on the Frauenplan, which was not then open to the public. We are told, however, that he was more interested in the Fröbel kindergarten, conducted by one of Fröbel's own pupils, and studied its pedagogic system with the greatest zeal and curiosity.

You see, of course, why I have told you this little tale. It was in hope to render more palatable the " and " at the top of the page, which must have made you lift your eyebrows at first sight. Goethe and Tolstoy. What sort of arbitrary and unseemly combination is that? Nietzsche once reproached us Germans with a peculiar clumsiness in the use of the word " and." We said " Schopenhauer and Hartmann," he sneered; we said " Goethe and Schiller " too — he was very much afraid we even said " Schiller and Goethe " ! Setting Schopenhauer and Hartmann aside; as far as Goethe and Schiller are concerned, Nietzsche's highly subjective dislike of moralists and theatre people should not have led him so far astray as to deny a relationship which is not less valid because of the inherent and typical contrast it displays. Its best spokesman, indeed, was its supposedly affronted half! It was hasty of Nietzsche, it was unjustifiably autocratic, thus to mock, and in his mockery to invoke, or assume, an order of merit which is, and must remain, highly controversial, the most controversial thing in the world. It is not on the whole the German way to be hasty in deciding precisely this question of all

6

questions. We instinctively avoid putting ourselves on record, on one side or the other. We prefer a free-handed policy, and so, personally, do I; and I mean to stick to this policy, to support and glorify it, in all that follows. Precisely this policy, and no other, is the meaning of the conjunction when we say " Goethe *and* Schiller ": where it converts the combination to an antithesis, and combines with the deliberate intention of contrast. No one who has ever come into contact with the sphere of German thought represented by that classic essay which comprehends all the others and makes them superfluous — I mean Schiller's *Naive und Sentimentalische Dichtung* — can fail to find this " and " deeply antithetic. Another precisely similar instance is the conjunction " Tolstoy *and* Dostoyevsky." On the other hand, if we deny the " and " its right to point a contrast, and confine its function to asserting essential affinity, essential similarity — what then? Would there not at once take place in our fancy a change of partners? On profound intellectual, nay, rather, on profoundly natural grounds, would not Schiller and Dostoyevsky move together, and on the other side — Goethe and Tolstoy?

You will be feeling far from satisfied. Obviously. You will say: there is something besides quality, there is position, there is rank. All honour, you will say, to antithesis, but things which differ so much in order of greatness really cannot be placed alongside like that. Granted that the one was a European humanist and thorough-paced pagan, while the other was an anarchist, and a primitive oriental Christian to boot. But the German world-poet, whose name

7

one names with the highest, with Dante, with Shakespeare, and the realistic novelist who in our own era and not so long ago ended his enigmatic life, and that truly in a most enigmatic manner; to speak of these two in the same breath — it simply will not do, it is an offence against the aristocratic instinct, it is in bad taste.

We put on one side the paganism of the one, the Christianity of the other. Let us leave them there — we may find time to come back to them later on. But as for this aristocratic instinct, if you like to call it that; let me say roundly that so far from offending against it with my parallel, I do it explicit honour. Are you certain you have no delusions — are you sure your perspective is not distorted in this matter of rank and relative greatness? Turgeniev, in his last letter to Tolstoy, written on his death-bed in Paris, in which he conjured his friend to return to literature and stop tormenting himself with theology, Turgeniev was the first to give Tolstoy the title of " the great writer of Russia," which he has had ever since, and which seems to mean that he holds in the eyes of his countrymen the same rank that the author of *Faust* and *Wilhelm Meister* does in ours. Tolstoy himself, as we were saying, was Christian through and through. Yet his humility was not so exaggerated as to prevent him from setting his name boldly beside the greatest, yes, beside the legendary great. He said of *War and Peace:* " Modesty aside, it is something like the Iliad." He was heard to say the same of his earliest work, *Childhood, Boyhood, Youth.* Was that megalomania? To me, frankly, it sounds like plain and simple fact. " *Nur die*

8

Lumpe," says Goethe, *" sind bescheiden."* A heathen saying. But Tolstoy subscribed to it. He saw himself always of
heroic grandeur; and as early as at thirty-seven, writing
in his diary, he ranked his own works, the finished and the
still to write, with the great literature of the world.

In the judgment, then, of those competent to render it,
the great writer of Russia; by his own estimate, the Homer
of his time — but that is not all. After Tolstoy's death
Maxim Gorky published a little book of reminiscences,
the best book, in my humble opinion, that he has written.
It closes with the words: " And I, who do not believe in
God, looked at him timidly, for some dark reason looked
at him and thought: The man is godlike." Godlike. Extraordinary. Nobody ever said or thought that of Dostoyevsky, nobody ever could have thought or said it. He has been
called a saint; and one might in all sincerity apply the
word to Schiller, at least in the Christian sense which it
must always connote, if without the specifically Byzantine
flavour. But Goethe and Tolstoy, these two, have been
found godlike. The epithet " Olympian " is a common-
place. It was not, however, only as a world-renowned old
man of commanding intellect that Goethe had it applied to
him; it was while he was still young, still the youth, of
whose godlike, compelling gaze Wieland sang, that he had
the attribute conferred upon him, a thousand times, by his
own contemporaries. Riemer relates that at sixty the old
man took occasion to make rather acridly merry over it.
" The deuce take godlike," he cried. " What good does it
do me to have people say: ' That is a godlike man,' when I

9

go by? They behave just as they like, they impose on me just the same. People only call a man godlike when he lets them have their own way! " — As for Tolstoy, you could not say he was Olympian; he was not a humanistic god, of course. He was, Gorky says, more like some sort of Russian god, sitting on a maple throne under a golden lime-tree; pagan, then, with a difference, compared with the Zeus of Weimar, but pagan none the less, because gods *are* pagan. Why? Because they are of the same essence as nature. One does not need to be a follower of Spinoza — as Goethe was, and had his own good reasons for it — to feel God and Nature as one, and the nobility that nature confers as godlike. "His superhumanly developed individuality is a monstrous phenomenon, almost forbidding, he has something in him of the fabled Sviatogor, whom the earth cannot hold." Thus Gorky, on Tolstoy. And I cite it in this matter of relative greatness. Gorky, for instance, goes on to say: " There is something about him which always makes me want to shout: ' Behold what a marvellous man lives upon this earth! ' For he is, so to speak, in general and beyond everything else, a human human being, a man." That sounds like something we have heard before. It reminds us of — whom?

No, the question of rank, the aristocratic problem, is no problem at all, within the grouping I have chosen. It becomes one only when we change partners: when we take saintly humanity and couple it, by means of the antithetic conjunction, with the godlike; when we say " Goethe and Schiller," " Tolstoy and Dostoyevsky." Only then, I think, do we pose the question of aristocracy, the problem in ethics and æsthetics: Which is greater? Which is more aristocratic? I shall not answer either of these. I will let the reader come to his individual conclusion in this matter of value, according to his own taste. Or, less glibly put, according to the conception he has of humanity, which — I must add, *sotto voce* — will have to be one-sided and incomplete to admit of his coming to any decision at all.

Is it not strangely moving to hear that one man had known them both, the creator of *Faust* and the " great writer of Russia " ? For certainly they belonged to different centuries. Tolstoy's life covered the greater part of the nineteenth. He is absolutely its son. As an artist he exhibits all of its characteristics, and, indeed, those of its second half. As for Goethe, the eighteenth century brought him forth, and essential traits of his character and training belong to it — a statement it would be very easy to substantiate. Yet on the other hand one might say that just as much of the eighteenth, Goethe's century, survived in Tolstoy as there had already come to birth of Tolstoy's, of the nineteenth, in Goethe. Tolstoy's rationalizing Christianity has more in common with the deism of the eighteenth century than it has with Dostoyevsky's violent and mystical religiosity, which was entirely of the nineteenth. His system of practical religion — the essence of which was a destructive intellectual force that undermined all regulations, human and divine — had more affinity with the social criticism of the eighteenth century than with Dostoyevsky's

11

moralizations, although those were, on the one hand, far more profound, on the other far more religious. And Tolstoy's *penchant* for Utopias, his hatred of civilization, his passion for rusticity, for a bucolic placidity of the soul — an aristocratic passion, the passion of a nobleman — to all that, the eighteenth century, and indeed the French eighteenth century, can lay claim. And, on the other hand, Goethe. What most astonishes us in that masterpiece of his old age, the sociological novel *Wilhelm Meisters Wanderjahre*, is the intuition, the keenness and breadth of vision — they seem positively occult, but are simply the expression of a finer organism, the fruit of the most sensitive penetration — which anticipate the whole social and economic development of the nineteenth century: the industrialization of the old cultural and agrarian countries, the triumph of the machine, the rise of the organized labouring classes, the class conflict, democracy, socialism, Americanism itself, with the intellectual and educational consequences of all these.

But when all is said, and whatever the chronological affinity of these two great men, they cannot be called contemporaries. Only four years did the two of them inhabit this mortal sphere together: from 1828, when Tolstoy was born, to 1832, when Goethe died. Which does not prevent them from having one cultural element of their intellectual and spiritual make-up in common, and that a very real and positive one — to say nothing of universally human elements like Homer and the Bible. I mean the element Rousseau.

12

" I have read the whole of Rousseau, the whole twenty volumes, including the lexicon of music. What I felt for him was more than enthusiasm; it was worship. At fifteen I wore round my neck, instead of the usual crucifix, a medallion with his picture. I am so familiar with some of the passages in his works that I feel as though I had written them myself." These are Tolstoy's words, taken from his *Confessions*. And certainly he was Rousseauian more intimately, more personally, more damagingly, so to speak, than was Goethe, who as a man had nothing in common with poor Jean Jacques's enigmatic and not always ingratiating complexities. Yet hear Goethe (I quote from an early review): " Religious conditions, and the social conditions so narrowly bound up with them; the pressure of the laws, the still greater pressure of society, to say nothing of a thousand other factors, leave the civilized man or the civilized nation no soul of his own. They stifle the promptings of nature, they obliterate every trait out of which a characteristic picture could be made." That is, from the literary point of view, *Sturm und Drang*. But from the intellectual and historical, it is Rousseauianism. It bears the impress of revolution, even of anarchy; though in the Russian seeker after God that impress is religious and early Christian, whereas in Goethe's words the humanistic trend can be felt, the irradiation of a cultural and self-developing individualism which Tolstoy would have banned as egoistic and unchristian. But unchristian, egoistic, it is not: it means work on man, on mankind, on humanity, and it issues, as the *Wanderjahre* shows, in the social world.

13

What two ideas does the very sound of Rousseau's name inevitably evoke — aside, that is, from the idea of nature, which is, of course, first and foremost? Why, naturally, the idea " education " and the idea " autobiography." Jean Jacques Rousseau was the author of *Émile* and of the *Confessions*. Now, both these elements, the pedagogic and the autobiographic, are present in full strength in Goethe as in Tolstoy; they cannot be dissociated from the work or the life of either. It is as an amateur pedagogue that Tolstoy has been introduced in this essay; and we know that for long years he was nothing else, that he forced into this channel the whole violence of the passion that was in him, and wrestled theoretically and practically to the very verge of exhaustion with the problem of the Russian primary school. As for Goethe, it is needless to say that his was a pedagogic nature in the fullest sense of the word. The two great monuments of his life, one in poetry and one in prose, the *Faust* and the *Wilhelm Meister*, are both creative treatments of the theme of education. And whereas in the *Lehrjahre* the idea is still that of the individual forming himself — " for to form myself, just as I am, was darkly, from my youth up, my purpose and my desire," says Wilhelm Meister — in the *Wanderjahre* the educational idea is objectivated, and issues in social, even in political concepts; while at the heart of the work is, as you know, the stern and beautiful Utopia of the *Pedagogic Province*.

The second association, the autobiographic, the confessional, is of course easy to attest in both authors. That all

14

of Goethe's works represent "fragments of one great confession" we should know ourselves even if he did not tell us; and is not *Dichtung und Wahrheit*, next to the *Confessions* of Saint Augustine and Rousseau, the most famous autobiography in the world? Well, and Tolstoy too wrote confessions: I mean in the main a book with that title, laid down throughout on the line of the great self-revelations that runs from the African saint to Strindberg, the son of the servant. But Tolstoy is in the same case with Goethe: not by virtue of one book alone is he autobiographical. Beginning with the *Childhood, Boyhood, Youth,* throughout the whole body of his work, he is autobiographical to an extent that makes it possible for Merezhkovsky, the great Russian critic, to say: " The artistic work of Leo Tolstoy is at bottom nothing else than one tremendous diary, kept for fifty years, one endless, explicit confession." Yes, and this critic adds: " In the literatures of all times and peoples there will hardly be found a second example of an author who reveals his personal and private life, often in its most intimate aspects, with such open-hearted sincerity." Well — open-hearted. . . . I may be allowed a comment upon the somewhat euphemistic epithet. One might, if one wanted to be invidious, use a different adjective to characterize this sincerity — an adjective that would suggest what Turgeniev had in mind when he once ironically referred to the shortcomings inevitable in a great writer: by which, obviously, he meant the lack of certain restraints, the absence of a customary reserve, discretion, decency, shame, or, on the positive side, the domination

15

of a definite claim on the love of the world — an absolute claim, indeed, in that it is all one to the revealer whether he reveal virtues or vices. He craves to be known and loved, loved because known, or loved *although* known; that is what I mean by an absolute claim on love. And the remarkable thing is that the world acknowledges and honours the claim.

" A life that is romantic has always self-love at the bottom of it." I like this saying; and subjoin that self-love is also always at the bottom of all autobiography. For the impulse a man feels to " fixate " his life, to exhibit its development, to celebrate his own destiny in set literary form and passionately invoke the sympathy of his contemporaries and posterity, has for a premise the same uncommonly lively sense of his own ego which, according to that penetrating saying, is at the bottom of a life full of romantic happenings. Subjectively, for the man himself, but also objectively for the world at large. Of course, this love of self is something different, something stronger, deeper, more fruitful, than any mere self-complacency or self-love of the ordinary kind. In the finest instances it is what Goethe in the *Wanderjahre* calls " *Ehrfurcht vor sich selbst*," and celebrates as the highest form of awe. It is the grateful and reverent self-absorption of the darling of the gods, that rings with incomparable sincerity from the lines:

> *Alles geben die Götter, die unendlichen,*
> *Ihren Lieblingen ganz:*
> *Alle Freuden, die unendlichen,*
> *Alle Schmerzen, die unendlichen, ganz.*

16

It is a proud and naïve interest in the mystery of high preferment, tangible superiority, perilous privilege, whose standard-bearer the chosen one feels himself to be; it is a craving to bear witness, out of the deeps of experience, how a genius is shaped; a desire to link together, by some miracle of grace, joy, and service; it was this desire which brought forth *Dichtung und Wahrheit* and in the truest sense inspires all great autobiography.

" I felt the need," writes Tolstoy of his youthful period, " to be known and loved of all the world; to *name my name,* the sound of which would greatly impress everybody, so that they would troop round me and thank me for something. . . ." That was quite early, before he had conceived any of his creative works or envisaged the idea of founding a new, practical, earthly, dogmaless religion — though this idea, according to his journal, had occurred to him by the time he was twenty-seven years old. His name, he feels, his mere name, Leo Tolstoy, this formula for his darkly and mightily stirring ego, should, as it were, serve notice to the world; whereby, for some reason as yet unknown, the world should be greatly impressed, and feel impelled to surround him in grateful throngs. Long after that, in 1883 — at about the same date that Tolstoy posed for an artist friend, sitting at his table and writing — he reads aloud to another friend and admirer, the one-time officer Tschertkof, from the manuscript of his just-completed personal revelations *What Does My Faith Consist In?* He reads from this manuscript a categorical reprobation of military service, on the grounds of his Christianity;

17

which so gratifies the ex-officer that he hears nothing else,
ceases to listen, and only rouses out of his absorption when
he hears, suddenly uttered, the reader's own name. Tolstoy,
coming to the end of his manuscript, had, with particular
clarity, says Tschertkof, enunciated the name signed underneath the text: "Leo Tolstoy."

Goethe once played a little literary hoax with his own
name, which I have always found singularly touching. You
will recall that in the *West-östliche Divan* he selected for
himself as the lover of Marianne Zuleika the name of
Hatem (the most richly giving and receiving one). The
choice betrays a blissful self-preoccupation. Now, in one
of the poems, a glorious one, he uses this name at the end
of a line, where, however, it does not rhyme as according
to the structure of the verse it should, and the name which
would rhyme if it stood there is another, is Goethe's own;
so that the reader involuntarily makes the substitution
mentally as he reads. "*Nur dies Herz,*" says the already
white-haired lover to the youthful beloved,

> "*Nur dies Herz, es ist von Dauer,*
> *Schwillt in Jugendlichstem Flor;*
> *Unter Schnee und Nebelschauer*
> *Rast ein Ätna dir hervor.*
> *Du beschämst wie Morgenröte*
> *Jener Gipfel ernste Wand,*
> *Und noch einmal fühlet Hatem*
> *Frühlingshauch und Sommerbrand.*"

"*Und noch einmal fühlet Goethe . . .*" With what de-
lightful playfulness the poet makes the reader eliminate

18

the name Hatem, which does not give the rhyme his ear
expects! The eastern masquerade is abandoned for autobiography, the ear confutes the eye, and Goethe's own
name, beloved of men and gods, emerges with peculiar
clarity, rhymed to perfection and irradiated by the most
beautiful thing the world of sense can show: the rosy
dawn.

May one call that " *Selbstgefälligkeit,*" that awestruck
sense of plenitude, of copious abundance, which pervades
the consciousness of the darling of the gods? Goethe all
his life had set his face against the affectation which might
condemn such a feeling. He let it be known that in his
opinion self-condemnation was the business of those who
had no ground for anything else. He even openly spoke a
good word for ordinary vanity, and said that the suppres-
sion of it would mean social decay, adding that the vain
man can never be entirely crude. Whereupon follows the
question: Is love of self ever quite distinguishable from
love of humanity?

> *Wie sie sich an mich verschwendet,*
> *Bin ich mir ein wertes Ich;*
> *Hätte sie sich weggewendet,*
> *Augenblicks verlör' ich mich.*

And is not young Tolstoy's dream of glory, his craving to
be known and loved, evidence of his love to the great *Thou*
of the world? Love of the ego and love of the world are
psychologically not to be divorced; which makes the old
question whether love is ever altruistic, and not utterly
egotistic, the most idle question in the world. In love, the

19

contradiction between egotism and altruism is abrogated quite.

From which it follows that the autobiographical impulse scarcely ever turns out to be a mere dilettante trifling. It seems to carry its own justification with it. Talent, generally speaking, is a ticklish, difficult conception; the point of which is really less whether a man *can do* something than whether a man *is* something. One might almost say that talent is nothing more or less than a high state of adequacy to one's lot in life. But whose life is it that possesses this dignity in the face of destiny? With brains and sensibility anything can be made out of any life, out of any life a romantic existence can be made. Differing in this from the pure poetic impulse, which so often rests upon sheer self-deception, the autobiographic, as it seems, always presupposes a degree of brains and sensibility which justifies it beforehand; so that it need only become productive to be certain of our sympathy. Hence the conclusion I drew: that if the world sanction the love of self, which is at the bottom of the impulse, it will as a rule respond to it as well.

" Behold, what a marvellous creature lives upon this earth! " Gorky, contemplating Tolstoy, utters this inward cry. And this cry it is to which all biography seeks to move the world. Any human life, given brains and sensibility, can be made interesting and sympathetic, even the most wretched. J. J. Rousseau was not precisely one's idea of a darling of the gods. The father of the French Revolution was an unhappy wretch, half or three-quarters mad, and probably a suicide. Certainly the blend of sensibility and catarrh of the bladder displayed in the *Confessions* is not, æsthetically speaking, to everybody's taste. Nevertheless, his self-exposure contains and constitutes a claim upon the love of the world, which has been so abundantly honoured, with so many tears, that really one might call poor Jean Jacques the well-beloved, *le bien-aimé*. And this world-wide emotional response he owes to his bond with nature — rather a one-sided bond, it must be owned, for certainly this fool of genius, this exhibitionistic world-shaker, was a stepchild of the All-Mother rather than one of her pets, an accident of birth instead of a god-given miracle of favour and preference. His relation to nature was sentimental in the fullest sense of the word, and the tale of his life swept over the world in a wave of sentiment, not to say sentimentality. Poor Jean Jacques!

No, not in this tone does one refer to the two whom men called godlike, divine; in whom, as we have seen, important traits of Rousseau's character are reproduced. For they were not sentimental, scarcely had they occasion to yearn for nature, they themselves were nature. Their bond with her was not one-sided, like Rousseau's — or if it was, then it was nature who loved them, her darlings, loved them and clung to them, while on their side they drew away, and strove to free themselves from her heavy and earth-bound domination; with indifferent success, it must be said, looking at them both singly and together. Goethe confesses: " So here I am, with all my thousand thoughts, sent back to be a child again, unacquainted with the moment, in darkness

21

about myself." And to Schiller, the singer of the highest freedom, he writes: " How great an advantage your sympathy and interest will be to me you will soon see, when you discover in me a sort of sluggishness and gloom which is stronger than myself." And yet we may agree that Goethe's highly humanistic effort to " convert the cloudy natural product into a clear image of itself (i.e., of reason) and so discharge the duty and the claim of existence," as Riemer with extraordinary beauty expresses it, was crowned with a purer success than the attempt of Count Leo Nikolaevich Tolstoy to transform his life into the holy life of our blessed father the Bojar Lev, as Gorky says. This process of making a Christian and a saint of himself, on the part of a human being and artist so loved of nature that she had endowed him with godlikeness, was, as an effort at spiritual regeneration, most inept. Anglo-Saxondom hailed it with acclaim, but, after all, the spectacle is painful rather than gratifying, compared with Goethe's high endeavour. For there is no conflict between nature and culture; the second only ennobles the first, it does not repudiate it. But Tolstoy's method was not the ennoblement but the renunciation of self, and that can quite easily become the most mortifying kind of deception. It is true that Goethe, at a certain stage in his development, called *Götz* the work of an undisciplined boy; but never did he so childishly and miserably calumniate his own art as the ageing Tolstoy did, when he regretted having written *Childhood, Boyhood, Youth,* the fruit of his fresh youthful vigour, condemning it as insincere, literary, sinful; or

22

when he spoke at large of " the artistic twaddle " that filled the twelve volumes of his works, and to which " people today ascribe an unmerited significance." That is what I call false self-renunciation, a clumsy attempt at spiritualization. Yet renounce himself as he would in words, his very existence gave him the lie; and Gorky looked at him, the patriarch with the " sly " little smile and the artist hands with their swollen veins, and thought to himself: " The man is godlike."

Weimar, and Yasnaya Polyana. There is no spot on earth today whence power streams out as once from these two, no shrine strong in grace, the resort of pilgrims, whither the longings and vague hopes of men, their need and craving to adore, turn as they did thitherward at the beginning of the nineteenth and the beginning of the twentieth century. We possess descriptions of the state Goethe kept in Weimar; when he, now no longer merely the creator of certain works of art, but a prince of life, the highest representative of European culture, civilization, and humanity, with his staff of secretaries, his higher aides and eager friends at his back, bore up, with that bestarred official dignity which the world enjoined upon him and behind which he hid the mysteries and abysses of his genius, against the onrushing tide of civilized humanity — princes, artists, youths, and rustics, to whom the consciousness of having been vouchsafed one glimpse of him might gild the rest of their lives; even though the great moment itself might and often did turn out to be a chilling

23

disappointment. In much the same way, I say, the little Russian village became, about 1900, the centre and nodal point, the shrine whose virtue was such that it drew all the world. The host of pilgrims was even more colourful, more international, more heterogeneous; for during the century communications had increased, the world had broadened out. South Africans, Americans, Japanese, Australians, natives of the Malay Peninsula, Siberian refugees, and Indian Brahmins, representatives of all the European nations, scholars, poets, artists, statesmen, governors, senators, students, military personages, workmen, peasants, French politicians, journalists of every stripe, from every country on the globe; and again youth, youth from all over the world. "Who does not go to him? " asks a Russian writer: " to greet him, to express sympathy with his ideas, to seek relief from tormenting problems." And his biographer Birukov says: " One and all they troop to this village and then go home to talk about the great words and great thoughts of the grey old seer who lives there."

" Great words and great thoughts." Of course. But it is quite likely the words and thoughts with which the prophet regaled them were not always so remarkable. Neither were Goethe's; out of sheer embarrassment he might fail to utter great things to those who waited on him. But it is a question whether people ever went to Weimar or to the village called " Bright Meadow " for the sake of the great words and thoughts they might perchance hear, or were led by a much more profound and elemental

24

craving. I shall be accused of mysticism if I say that the attraction such shrines possess for all the world, so that men promise themselves salvation from a visit, is not at all intellectual in its nature but something else entirely. " Elemental " is the only word for it. For Goethe's case, I may quote Wilhelm von Humboldt, who declared, a few days after the master's death, that the strangest thing of all was the way this man had exercised so powerful an influence, without as it were meaning to at all, unconsciously, unintentionally, by the mere fact of his existence; this, he says, quite apart from his intellectual activity as a thinker and poet, and as an outgrowth of his great and unique personality. Well and good. But, after all, we use the word " personality " when we want to express an idea which at bottom escapes definition. Personality is not immediately a matter of mind or spirit — nor yet of culture. Our conception of it is one which takes us outside the domain of the rational, into the sphere of the mystic and elemental, into the *natural* sphere. " A great nature " — that is another phrase we use in our effort to find a formula and a symbol which shall express power streaming forth and drawing the world to itself. But nature is not spirit; in fact, this antithesis is, I should say, the greatest of all antitheses. Gorky not only disbelieved in Tolstoy's Christian, Buddhistic, Chinese gospel of wisdom, he did not even believe that Tolstoy believed in it. And yet he gazed at him, and thought, in amaze: " The man is like God." It was not spirit, but nature, moved him to this inward cry. And when the pilgrims trooped to Weimar and " Bright

25

Meadow " the refreshment and quickening they dimly hoped for was not of the mind; it was the sight of and contact with great vital energy, with human nature richly endowed, with the lofty nobility of a beloved child of God. For one does not need to be a Spinozist, like Goethe, who had his own good reasons for being one, to hail the favourites of nature as the favourites of God.

Schiller, great sufferer though he was, was kinder, more human to his visitors. This we learn for instance from the actor Friederich, who says he left this glorious poet " more consoled," after having just previously taken a chill, to speak figuratively, at an audience on the Frauenplan. " Goethe's whole appearance," he goes on, " seemed measured and formal. I sought in vain a trait that betrayed the genial creator of *The Sorrows of Werther* or *Wilhelm Meisters Lehrjahre*. You can imagine how this frigid reception and unfriendly treatment put me off, it was so contrary to all my expectations. Dearly should I have liked to say to Goethe: ' What sort of graven image are you? It is impossible that you could have written the *Lehrjahre*.' But I choked it down." One is reminded of the Moscow worthy with whom Gorky drove away from Yasnaya Polyana: who for a long time could not get his breath at all, only kept ruefully smiling and ejaculating as in a daze: " Well, well, that was a cold douche! Gracious, but he's stiff! And I thought he was an anarchist! " Perhaps, even probably, if it had been Dostoyevsky he visited, he would have found him more anarchistic — in other words, less " stiff " — and would have parted from him " more

26

consoled," as did the good Friederich from the glorious Schiller, who even let Friederich recite to him.
On the other hand, neither Schiller's nor Dostoyevsky's
genius would have turned any odd corner of the
earth into a shrine for pilgrims. Anyhow, neither of them
lived long enough for that. They died too young, they did
not reach the patriarchal years of Goethe and Tolstoy,
nature denied them the dignity and consecration of great
age, she did not grant them to be characteristically fruitful
throughout all the stages of the human scene, to live a
whole and classic human life. True, it may be said that
the dignity that comes with length of days has nothing to
do with spirit. A greybeard may be stupid and ordinary;
yet men do regard with religious awe his white hair and
wrinkles; his is a natural nobility conferred by length of
years — but natural nobility is probably a pleonasm. Nobility is always natural. People are not ennobled, that is
rubbish; they are noble by birth, on the ground of their
flesh and blood. Nobility then is physical: on the body
and not on the mind all nobility has always laid the greatest stress. That may explain a certain strain of brutality
which has always been peculiar to human nobility. And is
there not something brutal too, in its way, heathenish,
sagalike, in the arrogant way Goethe sometimes boasted
of his vitality, his indestructibility? When he was eighty-
one he said to Soret: "Well, so Sömmering is dead. He
was barely a miserable five-and-seventy years old! What
poor things men are, not to be brave enough to hold out
longer than that! On that score I really must do justice

to that highly radical ass my friend Bentham; he is quite well preserved, and he is a few weeks older than I am myself! "

So Schiller and Dostoyevsky, to get back to them, were not vouchsafed the ennoblement that comes with length of days. They died comparatively young. Why? Well, because they were sick men, as everybody knows, both of them; one consumptive, the other epileptic. But I raise two questions: First, do we not feel that their illness was deeply founded in the very being of the two of them, an essential and typical trait of the kind of men they were? And second, does it not seem that in their case it is the disease itself that engenders or brings out a nobility sharply distinguished from that love of self and the autobiographical pride of birth which is part of its consummate sense of its own ego? Schiller's nobility and Dostoyevsky's nobility mean a quite different sort of deepening and heightening of their humanity — yes, of their *humanity*, in view of which does not disease appear precisely as an aristocratic attribute of heightened humanity? It follows then that the phrase " natural nobility " is no pleonasm after all; that there does exist another kind of nobility besides that conferred by nature on her favoured sons. Clearly there are two ways of heightening and enhancing human values: one exalts them up to the godlike, and is a gift of nature's grace; the other exalts them up to the saintly, by grace of another power, which stands opposed to her and means emancipation from her, eternal revolt from her. That other power is

28

the power of the spirit. But the question which of these two is higher, which kind of enhancement of human values is the nobler: this it is which I called the aristocratic problem.

Here, with all due reserve, a little philosophy of disease may not be out of place. Disease has two faces and a double relation to man and his human dignity. On the one hand it is hostile: by overstressing the physical, by throwing man back upon his body, it has a dehumanizing effect. On the other hand, it is possible to think and feel about illness as a highly dignified human phenomenon. It may be going too far to say that disease *is* spirit, or, which would sound very tendentious, that spirit is disease. Still, the two conceptions do have very much in common. For the spirit is pride; it is a wilful denial and contradiction of nature; it is detachment, withdrawal, estrangement from her. Spirit is that which distinguishes from all other forms of organic life this creature man, this being which is to such a high degree independent of her and hostile to her. And the question, the aristocratic problem, is this: is he not by just so much the more man, the more detached he is from nature — that is to say, the more diseased he is? For what can disease be, if not disjunction from nature? " *Tut der Finger dir weh,*" says Hebbel epigrammatically, " *schied er vom Leibe sich ab,*

Und die Säfte beginnen, im Gliede gesondert zu kreisen:
Aber so ist auch der Mensch, fürcht' ich, ein Schmerz
nur in Gott."

Was it not Nietzsche who called man " *das kranke Tier* " ?
What did he mean, if not that man is more than beast only

29

in the measure that he is ailing? In spirit, then, in disease, resides the dignity of man; and the genius of disease is more human than the genius of health.

You will deny that; you will not agree to have it so. But, in the first place, disease, as a philosophical term, is by no means a negation and a condemnation. It is merely a statement, which need be no less acceptable than the term "health," there being a nobility of disease as there is a nobility of health. And, in the second place, may I remind you that Goethe identified the Schillerian conception of the "sentimental" with that of disease? After, that is, he had previously identified the antithesis of "simple and sentimental" with that of classic and romantic. "The conception of classic and romantic poetry," he said one day to Eckermann, "that is abroad today, and making so much strife and schism, came originally from Schiller and me. My poetical maxim has been objectivity of treatment, and I wanted it to prevail. But Schiller, whose method is entirely subjective, thought his way was right, and wrote the essay on simple and sentimental poetry in defence of his conception." Again: "I have thought of a new phrase which states not too badly the relation between the classic and the romantic. The classic I call the healthy, the romantic the diseased. If we distinguish classic and romantic on this basis we shall soon clarify the situation."

Here, then, we have an order of things according to which, on the one hand, the simple, the objective, the sound, and the classic are identical; and, on the other hand, the "sentimental," the subjective, the pathological, the ro-

30

mantic. Thus one might call man the romantic being, in that he, a spiritual entity, stands outside of and beyond nature, and in this his emotional separation from her, in this his double essence of nature and spirit, finds both his own importance and his own misery. Nature is happy, or she seems so to him. For he, involved in tragical paradox, is a romantically miserable being. Does not all our love of our kind rest on a brotherly, sympathetic recognition of the human being's well-nigh hopelessly difficult situation? Yes, there is a patriotism of humanity, and it rests on this: we love human beings because they have such a hard time — and because we are one of them ourself!

Tolstoy, in his *Confessions,* remarks that as a small child he knew nothing of nature, he had not even noticed her existence. " It is not possible," he says, " that I was given neither flowers nor leaves to play with, that I did not see the grass or the sunlight. And yet up to my fifth or sixth year I have no memory of what we call nature. Probably we have to get free from her in order to see her, and I myself was nature." From which can be deduced that even the mere seeing of nature, and our so-called enjoyment of her, are not only a specifically human condition, but one full of yearning emotion, in other words pathological, implying as it does our separation from her. Tolstoy's recollection is that he felt the pain of this separation for the first time when his childhood under the care of nurses came to an end and he moved over to his older brothers and the tutor Feodor Ivanovich in the lower storey. Never again,

31

he assures us, did he feel so strongly what a sense of duty meant, and what, accordingly, moral and ethical obligation: " the feeling of the Cross, to carry which every one of us is called. It was hard for me to part from all I had known since I was born. I was sad, sunk in poetical melancholy; less because I had to part from human beings, my nurse, my sisters, my aunt, than because I was leaving my little bed with its curtains and pillows. Moreover, I was apprehensive of the new life I was entering." The appearance of the word " Cross " in this connexion is significant, not only with reference to Tolstoy, but also for the thing itself, the process of loosing oneself from nature. This process was felt by Tolstoy as painful and ethical: painful because ethical, and ethical because painful. He gives it a moral and an ascetic significance, as that which actually comprises all man's ethical obligation. To be humanized means, for him, to be denaturalized; and from that moment on, the struggle of his existence consists in this sort of humanizing process: in the divorce from nature, from everything that was natural and to him peculiarly so, for example from the family, the nation, the State, the Church, from all the passions of the senses and the instincts, from love, the hunt, at bottom from all of physical life, and especially from art, which meant to him quite essentially the life of the body and the senses. It is quite wrong to think of this struggle as a crisis of conversion taking place suddenly in his later years; to make its inception roughly coincide with the beginning of old age. When the news came that the great Russian writer was as though

32

stricken by a sort of mystical madness, the Frenchman Vogué declared that he had long expected it. He was quite justified. The germ of Tolstoy's intellectual development had lain in *Childhood, Boyhood, Youth;* and the psychology of Levin in *Anna Karenine* plainly indicated what further course it would take. Besides, we have the evidence of Tolstoy's comrades in arms when he was an officer, the Sebastopol time. They give the clearest picture of the violence with which the struggle even then raged within him. But here we should note that his wrestling to break the strong bonds in which nature held him, regularly led up to disease, immediately assumed the form of illness. " Leochen is completely consumed by his writing now," so his wife, Countess Sophia Alexandrovna, puts it, about the year 1880, when he buried himself in theology and the philosophy of religion. It is a sight her love hates to see, and she constantly tries to call him back to creative work. " His eyes are strange and staring, he hardly speaks at all, he is like a being from another world, and is positively not capable of thinking of earthly things. . . ." " Leochen is quite sunk in his work. His head pains him all the time. He is very much changed, and become a rigid and practising Christian. But he has got grey, his health is weak, he is sadder and more silent all the time." — " Tomorrow we shall have been here a month," she writes in 1881 from Moscow, " and the first two weeks I wept every day without stopping, because Leochen was not only in a gloomy state, but fallen into a kind of despairing apathy. He ate nothing and did not sleep, sometimes literally wept — I honestly believe I shall lose my reason." And to her husband himself: " I am beginning to think that when a happy man suddenly begins to see only the horrible side of life, and has no eyes for anything good, he must be ill. You should do something for it, I say this in all seriousness. It seems so clear to me, I suffer so to see you. . . . Did you never know before that there were people in the world who were hungry, miserable, unhappy, and wicked? Open your eyes: there are also strong and healthy, happy and good ones. If God would only help you — what can I do? You must be ill," the poor woman wails — and is he not? He himself writes: " My health grows worse and worse, often I wish I could die. Why I am so reduced, I do not know myself. Perhaps it is age, perhaps illness. . . ."

Compare with this the descriptions of him when he had sought in the holy animalism of married life a refuge from the insoluble riddles that his intellect set him; and then, with that power which the critics delighted to call " bear-like " — Turgeniev sought in vain to convince him that it came from the source whence all things come — created his two epic novels *War and Peace* and *Anna Karenine*. " He was always light-hearted then," his sister-in-law relates, " in high spirits, as the English say, fresh, healthy, and jolly. On the days when he did not write he went hunting with me or his neighbour Ribikov. We hunted with greyhounds. . . . Evenings he played patience in Tantchen's room." What happy days! Who can blame poor Countess Sophia Alexandrovna for scarcely containing herself for joy when she hears that her hollow-eyed Christian is planning a new imaginative work? Her happiness is touching. " What gladness suddenly filled me, to read that you mean to write something creative again! What I have so long awaited and hoped for has come to you. That is salvation, that is happiness, in it we shall come together again, it will console you and irradiate our life. This is the work you were made for, and outside this sphere there is no joy for your soul. God give you strength to cling to this ray of light, in order that the divine spark may flare up in you again. The thought fills me with ecstasy. . . ."

Goethe's and Tolstoy's biographies show that these great writers both alike suppressed for years their gift of plastic creation — for which, as Countess Sophia Alexandrovna says, they were born — and both in the service of a directly social activity — that is to say, on highly moral grounds. Tolstoy suppressed the artist in him in favour of his activities as *mirowov posrednik* (justice of the peace) and schoolmaster without pay. Goethe governed the dukedom of Saxe-Weimar, for ten years of his early manhood dedicated his powers to excise regulations, details of book manufacture, levies of recruits, construction of streets and water-conduits, workhouses, mines and quarries, finance, and other such matters — while Merck, in the style of Turgeniev, was constantly concerned to rescue him for literature, and he himself, with increasing resignation, steeling himself by inward exhortations to patience and fortitude, held himself to the heavy, hard, unrewarding, unnatural task. Added to all this, in Goethe's case, there was that somewhat seraphic affair with Frau von Stein. No

35

doubt it was most beautifully instrumental in the process of civilizing the son of the Titans; but after all it did justice to but one of those famous two souls, which had, alas, their dwelling in his breast, and it let the other, the one with the "*klammernde Organen*," the "prehensile organs," go empty away. — Well, in both cases, Goethe's and Tolstoy's, the result is illness. "My office as justice of the peace," writes Tolstoy, "has ended in destroying my good relations with the landowners, quite aside from the fact that it injures my health." Teaching the village children had the same result. True, in his pedagogical journal he claims that the exercises the children wrote were more accomplished than the writings of Leo Tolstoy, Pushkin, and Goethe; yet he discerns something evil and even criminal in his intercourse with them, it seems to him that he abuses and corrupts their souls. "It seemed to go very well," he says in the *Confessions*, "but I felt that I was mentally not healthy enough and that it could not go on so for much longer. I was more ailing mentally than physically; I threw it all overboard and drove out to the Kalmucks of the steppes to drink mares' milk and lead an animal life." — This absconding to the steppes vividly recalls the secret flight to Italy which was Goethe's salvation, after he too had seen that it could not go on so for much longer. The thirty-four-year-old man had become silent, taciturn, in plain words melancholy. He thought it was probably natural that a man should become serious over serious things. His health was actually undermined; by the time he was six-and-thirty his face was the face of a victim of exhaustion.

For the first time he thought of taking a cure. He began to be aware of the ruinous perversity of his existence; expressed his view in the shrewd understatement that he was meant for private life. And fled before destruction. The parallel continues to hold: for Leo Nikolaevich, returned from the steppes and the mares' milk cure, marries his Sophia Alexandrovna, who from then on finds herself almost continuously in the family way, and with epic and primeval power creates his two great novels. While Goethe, back from Italy, takes Christiane Vulpius unto himself and, freed from the cares of office, gives his mind to his natural tasks. All which might serve as a gloss upon a philosophy of disease.

Art is objective, creative contemplation, closely bound up with nature. Critique, on the other hand, is the moralizing, analysing attitude toward life and nature. In other words, critique is spirit; whereas creation is the preoccupation of the children of God and nature.

" In poetry my maxim was the objective principle," says Goethe. " I am a plastic artist." Indeed, the contrast between Goethe's position and that of his great counterpart (Schiller standing for idealism, moralization, rhetoric, in short for critique) is too well known to need labouring. Goethe regarded his own inborn poetic gift " quite as nature." His tolerance, his attitude of live and let live, the complaisance of his character, are all consonant with this view. They are based on the Spinozan concept of the perfectitude and necessity of all being, on the idea of a world free from final ends and final causes, in which evil has its rights like good. " We struggle," he declares, " to perfect the work of art as an end in itself. They, the moralists, think of the ulterior effect, about which the true artist troubles himself as little as nature does when she makes a lion or a humming-bird." It is a primary maxim with him that art is as inimical to purpose as nature herself; and this is the point where the follower of Spinoza sympathizes with Kant, who conceives detached contemplation as the genuine æsthetic state, thus making a fundamental distinction between the æsthetic-creative principle and the ethical-critical one. " When," says Goethe, " philosophy confirms and enhances our original feeling of our oneness with nature, turning it into a profound and tranquil contemplation, then I welcome it." I could cite ten or twelve other places in his works, where in the name of art he repudiates the moral sanction — which indeed is always social as well. " It is possible, I suppose, for a work of art to have a moral effect; but to demand from the artist a moral purpose and intention is to spoil his craft for him." — " I have, in my trade as a writer, never asked myself: How shall I be of service to the world at large? All I have ever done was with the view of making myself better and more full of insight, of increasing the content of my own personality; and then only of giving utterance to what I had recognized as the good and the true."

When we contrast the Christian-social ethics of Tolstoy as an old man with Goethe's pagan and cultural idealism, we must not forget that the Tolstoyan socialism had its

38

origin in the most private and personal need, the profoundest concern with the salvation of one's own soul. A permanent dissatisfaction with self, a tortured seeking for the
meaning of life, was the source of this socialism. The
moralist began all his teachings and reforms with a self-
discipline (the *Confessions,* that is) such as the true and
proper social critic never demands of himself. Revolutionary in the real and political sense of the word he can by
no means be called. " The significance of the Christian
doctrine," he declares, " is not that in its name society
shall forcibly be reformed. It is that one shall find a meaning to life." And it should be pointed out that Tolstoy's
original conception of art corresponded precisely to
Goethe's — a fact which will surprise none but those who
in all good faith accept him as a child of spirit, like Schiller
and Dostoyevsky, on the ground of his naïve and clumsy
efforts at spiritual regeneration, and fail to recognize in
him a natural nobility akin to Goethe's own. Tolstoy's
hatred of Shakespeare, which dates from much earlier than
is generally realized, undoubtedly has its roots in antagonism against that universal and all-accepting nature: in the
jealousy which a man enduring moral torment was bound
to feel in face of the blithe irony of an absolutely creative
genius. It was a reaction against nature, against the simple,
against indifference to the moral point of view; and an impulse toward spirit — that is, toward an ethical and even
social revaluation — a reaction so whole-souled, indeed,
that it ended in his playing off against Shakespeare Mrs.
Harriet Beecher Stowe, the creator of *Uncle Tom's Cabin*

— an absurdity which only goes to show how very much the child of nature he was. Genuine sons of spirit and of the idea, like Schiller and Dostoyevsky, do not run aground on such fantastic coasts. Tolstoy's critical and moral faculty, in short his bias toward spirit, was but a secondary impulse, and a feeble one at that. It always balked at organic union with his mighty creative gift; we have unequivocal declarations from him to the effect that, in his view, pure creative power stood higher than talent with a social coloration. As an old man he criticized Dostoyevsky for going in for politics, much as Goethe had criticized Uhland's activities in that line. At the age of thirty-one, in 1859, as a member of the Moscow society of the Friends of Russian Literature, he made a speech in which he so sharply accented the superiority of the purely artistic elements in literature over merits due to ulterior or ephemeral causes that the president of the society, Chomiakof, reminded him in a sharp rejoinder that a servant of pure art might very well, without knowing or wishing it, find himself indicting society.

An outburst of intellectual misgivings, of that humility of spirit to which the sons of nature are prone, occurs at the end of Tolstoy's novel *Lucerne*. Here is a splendid lament over the fate of man, who, with all his need of positive redemption, is flung into an ever-billowing and shoreless ocean of good and evil. " If man," cries Tolstoy, " had only once learned not to judge and think so sharply and decisively, and not always to give answers to questions which are only put in order that they may remain for ever questions! If he would only comprehend that every thought

40

is at once false and true! . . . Men have divided up into sections this ever-rolling, boundless, eternally mingled chaos of good and bad; they have drawn themselves imaginary boundary-lines in this sea, and they expect the sea to divide according to their lines. As if it were not possible to make millions of other divisions, from other points of view, and on different planes! . . . Civilization is good, barbarism evil, freedom is good, unfreedom evil. This imaginary knowledge destroys in human nature the *original blissful and instinctive striving towards good.*" And asking himself whether in the souls of the poor there may not be more happiness and affirmation of life than in that of the callous rich man against whom, for his own part, his heart revolts, he bursts out with the words: " Endless is the goodness and wisdom of Him who has permitted and commanded all these contradictions. Only to you, poor worm, so presumptuously struggling to accomplish your schemes and devices, only to you do they seem contradictory. He looks mildly down from His radiant, immeasurable height and rejoices in the endless harmony wherein in endless conflict you all do move! "

Could one express oneself more " Goethically " ? Even the " *Harmonie des Unendlichen* " is here. This is not mere philosophical or moral doubt; the words are too light, too thin, too intellectual to characterize the piety, the religious submission, the adoration of nature, that breathe from Tolstoy's page. This is not the voice of the prophet, schoolmaster, and reformer; here speaks the child of this world, the creative artist. Nature was his element, as she was the

41

element, the beloved, kindly mother, of Goethe — and his
constant tearing at the bond which held him fast to her, his
desperate urging away from her in the direction of spirit
and morality, from creation to critique, has much to
command our respect and reverence, though at the same
time there is about it something painful, tormenting, and
humiliating, which is not present in the character of Goethe.
Look at Tolstoy's attitude toward music, it is most instructive. When he met Berthold Auerbach in Dresden, that not
too profound moralist told him that music is an irresponsible enjoyment, and added that irresponsible enjoyment is
the first step toward immorality. Tolstoy, in his journal,
made this clever and abominable phrase his own. His hatred
and fear of music had the same moral and social basis as
his hatred and fear of Shakespeare. We are told that at
the sound of music he grew pale and his face became drawn
with an expression very like horror. Notwithstanding, he
was never able to live without music. In his earlier years
he even founded a musical society. Before beginning work
he habitually seated himself at the piano — that means a
good deal. And in Moscow, when he sat beside Tschai-
kowsky and listened to the composer's Quartet in D major,
he began to sob at the *andante*, before everybody. No, un-
musical he was not. Music loved him, even though he, great
moralizing infant that he was, felt that he ought not to return her love.

There is that legend of the giant Antæus, who was unconquerable because fresh strength streamed into him whenever he touched his mother earth. The lives of Goethe and

Tolstoy irresistibly recall that myth. Both sons of mother earth, they differ only therein, that one of them was aware of the source of his nobility, the other not. There are places in Tolstoy's remorseful confessions where he touches the earth, and all at once his words, which, so long as they dealt in theory, were wooden and confused, are imbued with the most penetrating sensuousness, with an irresistible force and freshness of life. He recalls how once as a child he went nutting with his grandmother in the hazel-wood. Lackeys instead of horses draw the grandmother's little carriage into the grove. They break through the undergrowth and bend the boughs, full of ripe, already dropping nuts, down into the old lady's lap and she gathers them into a bag. Little Leo marvels at the strength of the tutor, Feodor Ivanovich, who bends the heavy branches; when he lets go they spring up again and slowly mingle with the others. " I can feel how hot it was in the sun, how pleasantly cool in the shade, how we breathed the sharp scent of the hazel leaves, while all round us the girls were cracking nuts between their teeth; we munched the full, fresh, white kernels without stopping." — The fresh, full, white kernels cracking between the girls' teeth: that is Antæus-Tolstoy, and the strength of his mother the earth streams through him, as it did when he wrote *War and Peace*, where his rather vague, fine-drawn, not very convincing philosophical digressions are followed by pages of which Turgeniev wrote: " They are glorious, they are the very best there is, everything original, everything descriptive, the hunt, the night boat-ride and all — nobody in Europe can touch him."

And Goethe: how the Antæus-consciousness governed his whole existence! How constantly it conditioned his seeking and shaping! Nature is to him "healing and comfort" after the visitations of passion; and while he well knows that to know her "one must have moulded all the manifestations of the human being into one definite and distinct entity," that true research is unthinkable without the gift of imagination, he is wary of the fantastic, avoids speculative natural philosophy, guards himself against losing touch with the earth, and calls the idea "the result of experience." The imagination that guides his research is intuitive, it is the inborn sympathy of the child of nature with the organic. It is Antæan, like the imaginative power which conditions his creative art, nor is that, either, capricious in its nature, but precise and based on the sense-perceptions. Such is the imagination of the creative artist. The sons of the thought, of the idea, of spirit, theirs is another kind. We will not say that the one creates more reality than the other. But the figures created by the plastic fancy possess the realism of sheer being; while those created by the "sentimental" artist evince their actuality by action. Schiller himself makes this distinction. Apart from the things they do, he himself confesses, they have something shadowy — "etwas Schattenhaftes" is his expression. Translate this from the sphere of German idealism into the Russian and revelational, and you get, as a sort of national pendant to Schiller's world of idea, rhetoric, and drama, the shadow-world of Dostoyevsky, over-life-size and exaggeratedly true. A catchword occurs to one from the philosophy of art, that is in everybody's mouth today, or at least was yesterday: the word "expressionism." Really, what we call expressionism is only a late form, strongly impregnated with the Russian and revelational, of romantic idealism. Its conflict with the epic attitude toward art, the conflict between contemplation and ecstatic vision, is neither new nor old, it is eternal. And it finds complete expression in on the one side Goethe and Tolstoy, on the other Schiller and Dostoyevsky. And to all eternity the truth, power, calm, and humility of nature will be in conflict with the disproportionate, fevered, and dogmatic presumption of spirit.

Very much, yes, precisely as Goethe's "profound and tranquil contemplation," his precise and sensuous fancy, the lifelikeness of his characters, stand in relation to the ideal visions of Schiller and the activism of his creations, so the mighty sense-appeal of Tolstoy's art stands to Dostoyevsky's sickly, distorted dream-and-soul world. Indeed, the contrast becomes even more pointed by reason of differences between nations and periods. Tolstoy, the realistic novelist, the prince-and-peasant scion of a race still young, displays in his art a sensuousness more powerful, more immediately fleshly in its appeal, than does the German humanist and classicist, bourgeois-born and patrician-bred, in his.

Compared with Eduard and Charlotte, the lovers in the *Wahlverwandtschaften*, Vronsky and Anna are like a fine strong stallion and a noble mare. The comparison is not

45

mine; it has often been made. A certain school of Russian criticism, hostile, of course, and on a low plane, found most offensive Tolstoy's animalism, his unheard-of interest in the life of the body, his genius for bringing home to us man's physical being. These critics wrote, for instance, that *Anna Karenine* reeked with the classic odour of babies' diapers. They raved at the salaciousness of certain scenes, and ironically reproached Tolstoy for omitting to describe how Anna takes her bath and Vronsky washes himself. They were wrong even in the fact; for Tolstoy does tell us how Vronsky washes, we see him rubbing his red body. And in *War and Peace* we are vouchsafed a glimpse of Napoleon naked, in the scene where he has his fat back sprayed with eau-de-Cologne. A critic wrote in *Die Tat* about this book: " Its main theme is the satisfaction of any and every human being within the fold of wedded bliss, conceived in the grossest sense." And then the same critic, parodying Tolstoy's style, proposed to him that he write another novel treating of Levin's love for his cow Pania.

All this, of course, is on a lower plane than the criticism of Goethe which Caroline Herder wrote to Knebel: " Oh, if he would only give some soul to his characters! If only there were not so much philandering in everything that he writes, or, as he himself so likes to call it, so much ' good feeling.' " But unenlightened comment such as this may very well be illuminating none the less, even though unawares and as it were on false pretences; and these remarks, in their folly, do undoubtedly contain a grain of truth. Caroline's " philandering " is a mincing, sentimental word

46

to characterize what Goethe wrote; yet it has a certain apt-
ness, if the comparison is between his frank realism and the
lofty insubstantiality of Schiller's world. It is not such a
bad joke, either, to make Levin fall in love with his cow. It
hits off the fleshliness of Tolstoy's art as contrasted with
the holy soulfulness of Dostoyevsky's — especially when
we remember Tolstoy's personal passion for one of the pre-
occupations of farm life — namely, the breeding of cattle
and pigs. It is an interest quite proper, of course, to a
landed proprietor; yet where so strongly marked as this
surely not quite without deeper meaning.

I am still resolved not to pass judgment. I did, indeed,
throw out the question of nobility, the matter of rank. But
I am wary of hasty decisions, and even at the risk of being
called vacillating, I hold to my policy of the free hand and
my faith in its ultimate fruitfulness. Why should I not be
a cautious judge of the swaying battle, when I know
that what I called above the arrogance of spirit is one
with that great and highly affecting principle which we call
freedom?

Schiller's loftiest boast is the freedom of the singer. But
Goethe's attitude toward the conception of freedom is at
all times cautious, not only in the political field, but con-
sistently, fundamentally, and in every connexion. Of
Schiller he says: " In his latter years, when he had had
enough of freedom in a physical sense, he went over to
it in the realm of the ideal, and I might almost say that
it killed him; for it caused him to make demands on his

physical powers that were altogether too much for them.
I have great respect for the categorical imperative, I know
how much good can come of it; but one must not carry it
too far, for then this idea of the ideal freedom certainly
leads to no good." — I confess that this habit of using
Schiller's heroic life to point a warning against exaggera-
tions in the use of the categorical imperative has always
made me smile. To confront the moral with the natural is
always humorous. But in other places where this child of
God expresses himself about heroes and saints his words
have quite a different ring and bear witness frankly and
sincerely to the nobility of spirit. He declared one day that
he passed for an aristocrat, but that Schiller was at bottom
much more of a one than he. The remark bears directly
upon the problem of aristocracy: certainly not in the political field, nor yet to the fact that Schiller had spoken of the
" eternally blind," to whom one must not lend Heaven's
torches of light; no, it has immediate reference to the aristocracy of spirit, which Goethe was at the moment compar-
ing with his own, the aristocracy of nature, and finding
it the more lofty of the two. " Nothing disturbed him," he
says admiringly, " nothing constrained him, nothing dis-
tracted the flight of his thoughts. He was as great at the
tea-table as he would have been in the council-chamber."
This admiring wonder rises from the depths of Goethe's
Antæus-nature, which had no consciousness at all of a
freedom like that, of such independence and unrestraint.
Rather he knew himself to be constantly conditioned by a
hundred circumstances; influenced, obligated, willingly

indeed, with a certain pride in his earth-bound aristocracy, yet influenced and obligated none the less. Pantheistic necessity was the fundamental feeling of his existence. It is not enough to say he did not believe in the freedom of the will. He denied the conception, he denied that such a thing was even conceivable. " We belong to the laws of nature," he says, " even when we rebel against them; we are working with her, even when we work against her." That dæmonic determinism of his whole being was often felt by others. They said he was possessed, and not able to act voluntarily. His earth-bound state manifested itself, for instance, in such sensitiveness to weather that he called himself a regular barometer. And we may not take it that he felt his dependence, which amounted to compulsion, as personally lowering, or that his will had ever rebelled against it. The will is the spirit: nature is by way of being mild and easy-going. Thus the aristocrat in bondage may feel a noble pride as he bends the knee to the dark power to which he belongs and which guides him so well; and yet be capable, as Goethe's case shows at least, of a gesture of elegant homage before the aristocracy of freedom. " *Denn hinter ihm,*" says Goethe in the Epilogue to *The Bell,* with reference to Schiller:

> *Denn hinter ihm in wesenlosem Scheine*
> *Lag, was uns alle bändigt, das Gemeine.*

Truly this is homage which breathes a spirit of the most profound resignation. For what *is* " *das Gemeine* " ? Nothing else than the natural, from the point of view of spirit and of freedom. For freedom is spirit; it is release

49

from nature, rebellion against her; it is humanity conceived as emancipation from the natural and its bondage, this emancipation being the thing that is actually human and worthy of humanity. Here we see the question of aristocracy flowing together with that of human dignity. Which is finer, which worthier of humanity, freedom or bonds, self-will or submission, the moral or the natural? If I refuse to answer, it is in the conviction that this question can never be answered with finality.

But, on the other hand, the moral " sentimentalist " can be no " sentimentalist " at all if he does not on his side display an even livelier and profounder eagerness to pay homage to the aristocracy which is of nature. Unquestionably there is a certain charming humility in the attitude of spirit toward nature, a delicate readiness, often quite unrequited, to pay her respect, which is one of the greatest and most touching phenomena of the higher life. Dostoyevsky read Tolstoy's early work *Childhood, Boyhood, Youth* in Siberia, in the periodical called *The Contemporary*, and was so taken with it that he inquired on all sides after the anonymous author. " Calm, deep, clear, yet unfathomable as nature is unfathomable, that is the impression it leaves," he writes. " There it is, and everything, even the smallest detail, shows the beautiful unity of the temperament from which it flows." — No, these are not Dostoyevsky's words, though they might have been. It is Schiller who writes thus, about *Wilhelm Meister*, in that letter in which, for the first time, he apostrophizes Goethe as " Dearest Friend ": an emotional form of address, in which, so

50

far as I know, Goethe never explicitly acquiesced. Dostoyevsky wrote the profoundest and most loving of all existing critiques of *Anna Karenine;* a masterpiece of enthusiastic exposition, which Tolstoy, perhaps, never even read
(he never did read criticisms of his works), to say nothing
of his ever feeling impelled to write reviews of anything
by Dostoyevsky. When Feodor Michaelovich died, Tolstoy
is said to have said: " I loved that man very much." But
his consciousness of the fact came a little late in the day;
for while Dostoyevsky was alive Tolstoy never troubled
his head about him; while afterwards, in a letter to Strachof,
Dostoyevsky's biographer, he compared him with a horse,
who seemed a splendid creature and worth a thousand
roubles, until suddenly he went lame, and then the fine
strong animal was not worth a groschen. " The longer I
live," he said, " the more I think of men who are not lame."
But this horse-philosophy, as applied to the author of *The
Brothers Karamazof* does not seem quite happy, to put it
mildly.

We know, and we rejoice to know, that in the case of
Goethe and Schiller nature's attitude to spirit was altogether
more brotherly and dignified, and on a higher plane. But
if Goethe played here too the part of Hatem, the richly
bestowing and receiving one, he did not after all take from
the dear friend more than he gave him, to say nothing of all
he gave by virtue of his mere existence, unconsciously, involuntarily. Was not Schiller's part in the relationship,
after all, that of service? I think so, myself, simply because
it lies in the nature of the thing, because Schiller did not

in the least need, to keep him fruitful, the meed of praise, love, inspiration, which he bestowed upon Goethe. And I note that such a letter as his famous first one, which knit the bond between them, in which with kindly hand he " gave the sum " of Goethe's life, he never did get from Goethe in return.

One utterance of Schiller's to Goethe has always delighted me, it seems to characterize the relationship so wonderfully. I mean the passage in a letter where he warns Goethe against Kant, his own spiritual master and his idol. Goethe, he tells him, can only be a Spinozan; his beautiful simple nature would be at once vitiated by contact with a philosophy of freedom. It is no more and no less than the problem of irony which we catch sight of here: without exception the profoundest and most fascinating in the world. For we see here that nothing is more foreign to spirit than a desire to convert nature to itself. It warns nature against itself. To the moral " sentimentalist," all that is nature seems beautiful and highly worth preserving. Knowledge feels that life is beautiful; and this is the feeling of the moral for the simple, of the holy for the divine, of nature for spirit; and in this peculiarly absolute judgment of values resides the ironic god, resides Eros. Spirit accordingly enters into a relationship with nature which is in a sense erotic, in a sense determined by male-female sex-polarity. And by virtue of the relation it can venture to abase itself and dare the ultimate self-surrender, without thereby resigning any of its own nobility. Indeed, it will always retain the accent of a certain tender contempt.

In Hölderlin's lines precisely this emotional irony is immortalized:

Wer das Tiefste gedacht, liebt das Lebendigste,
Hohe Tugend versteht, wer in die Welt geblickt,
Und es neigen die Weisen
Oft am Ende zu Schönem sich.

On the other hand, this simple nature too has an ironic mood, which is one with the objectivity of its character and precisely coincides with the conception of poetry, inasmuch as it lifts itself above its subject, above joy and grief, good and bad, death and life, to play freely with them. Goethe speaks of this mood in *Dichtung und Wahrheit,* with reference to Herder.

It is plain that what kept Goethe apart from Schiller so long was, more than anything else, the latter's prepossessions on the subject of freedom: his conception of human dignity, which was entirely based on the dictatorship of spirit — that is, was entirely revolutionary in character — which conceived in this emancipated sense all humanity, all nobility, all human nobility — and that, to a nature like Goethe's, must have seemed both odious and insulting to nature. It is, for instance, certain *a priori* that Goethe took the greatest umbrage at the famous essay *Über Anmut und Würde.* In it occur things like the following: " Movements which have as principle only animal sensuousness belong only, however voluntary we may suppose them to be, to physical nature, which never reaches of itself to grace. If it were possible to have grace in the manifestations of physical appetites and instincts, grace would no longer be either capable or worthy to serve as the expression of humanity." That one might describe as idealistic malice of spirit against nature, and so Goethe must have regarded it. For it is audacious to assert that grace cannot come out of the sensuous, nor nature reach to grace. Grace, then, is not a manifestation worthy of humanity; for that desire can express itself with charm, and instinct with grace, is a " charming " fact of experience. And when Schiller goes on to say: " Grace is a beauty not given by nature, but produced by the subject itself . . . it is the beauty of form under the influence of free will; it is the beauty of those particular phenomena which the person himself determines. The architectonic beauty does honour to the author of nature; grace does honour to him who possesses it. That is a gift, this is a personal merit " — the moral distinction he draws between talent and personal merit becomes a consummate affront to Goethe's vital consciousness and his aristocratic feeling. " Fools never think," says Goethe, " how fortune and merit are linked together." What he means by " fortune " is what Schiller calls " nature " and " talent," and distinguishes from free human merit. While Goethe, half-maliciously, half-paradoxically going about to deprive the word " merit " of the moralistic flavour that clings to it, likes to talk about " inborn merit." Everybody is free to call this a logical contradiction. But there are cases where logic is confronted by a metaphysical certainty higher than itself; and Goethe, who on the whole was certainly no metaphysician, undoubtedly felt the problem of freedom to be a metaphysical one.

54

That is to say, an undemonstrable intuition told him that
freedom, and therewith merit and demerit, were not a matter of the empirical but of the intelligible world; that, to
speak with Schopenhauer, freedom does not consist in
operari but in *esse*. Herein lies the humbleness of his aristocracy, the aristocracy of his humility; both of them so
categorically opposed to Schiller's idealistic evaluations,
his personal and moral pride in his freedom. Goethe, when
he wants to characterize the principle which composes his
essential nature, speaks humbly and gratefully of a " gift
of fortune." But the conception of a " gift," of " grace,"
is more aristocratic than one might think. What it means
is the indissoluble union of fortune and merit, a synthesis
of freedom and necessity, in short " inborn merit "; and
the gratitude, the humility, carry with them that metaphysical consciousness of being at all times and absolutely
certain of the favour of destiny.

There is, in Goethe's case, an amazing bit of evidence
on this point, which I cannot refrain from quoting. Speaking of Bentham, he says it is the height of madness for
the man, at his age, to be so radical. He is answered that
if His Excellence had been born in England he could
hardly have escaped being a radical and reformer. Whereat
Goethe, with Mephistophelian mien: " What do you take me
for? You think I would be spying out abuses and tacking
names on to them? I, who if I had been born in England
would have been living on abuses? If I had been born in
England I should have been a duke, or better still a bishop
with revenues of thirty thousand pounds sterling." —

" Very fine. But suppose Your Excellence had not drawn the big prize in the lottery; suppose you had drawn a blank? " To which Goethe: " Not everybody, my dear friend, is *made for the big prize*. Do you think I should have played such a foolish trick (*sottise*) as to draw a blank? "

All that, of course, is in jest. But is it only in jest? Does it not rather voice that deep metaphysical certainty that never and under no circumstances should he or could he be other than favoured and privileged, ever other than well-born? And in this certainty is there not after all something like a consciousness of freedom of the will, if only of freedom after the event? Really, it is priceless. To be born into the world a starving revolutionary, an idealistic " sentimentalist," that he calls a *sottise*. Is that the irony the children of God wreak on the children of spirit? If there be such a thing as inborn merit, then there is inborn demerit as well; and if it is a *sottise* to come into the world an average man, or poor, or sick, or stupid, then the criminal is indeed not only empirically but metaphysically culpable. For merit and reward, guilt and punishment, are conceptions that belong together. And one punishment at least, all those merit who have committed the *sottise* of drawing a blank in life's lottery: that of eternal destruction; whereas the chosen ones get eternal life too at the end. " *Wer keinen Namen sich erwarb, noch Edles will, gehört den Elementen an; so fahret hin!* " But as the possibility of nobly aspiring and achieving a name is not a matter of empirical freedom of the will, this " *so fahret hin* " is a piece of gross heartlessness. And if the conception of election by grace, to which that of metaphysical depravity corresponds, is a Christian conception, at any rate it shows Christianity turning its aristocratic side outwards.

I said awhile back that it seemed to me not accidental that Schiller and Dostoyevsky were sick men and did not, like Goethe and Tolstoy, arrive at a reverend length of days. Rather I was inclined to regard their poor health as fundamental to their characters. Quite as symbolic is the further external fact, that the two great realists and creative artists were of upper station, born to a privileged social status, whereas the heroes and saints of the idea, Schiller and Dostoyevsky, one the son of a Swabian army surgeon and the other of a Moscow hospital physician, were the children of modest people and spent all their days in pinched and homely, one might almost say undignified circumstances. I call this biographical fact symbolic, because it testifies to the Christianity of the spirit, whose kingdom, as the Scriptures say, is not of this world — in personalities as little as in the realm of the ideal and the artistic. Wherein it opposes a perpetual contrast to the kingdom of nature and nature's favourites, whose rank and essence are quite and entirely " of this world," the physical, pagan world. Therein lies their " realism." And they were, both Tolstoy and Goethe, realists enough to feel a naïve enjoyment in their privileged status, yes, in a sort to lay stress upon it and show themselves imbued by a consciousness of it; which would impress one as curiously unenlightened were it not plain that they themselves regard it in a symbolic sense and even rather childishly assimilate it in their own minds to their consciousness of their higher, extra-social, human aristocracy. Goethe's patrician birth was so dear to him that his patent of nobility, when he had it in his hands, meant " nothing, simply nothing." "We Frankfort patricians," he said, " always felt ourselves like nobility." But in the same conversation and connexion, by way of refuting a slur upon himself as the obsequious servant of royalty, he puts it thus: " Yes, I felt so much at ease (*so wohl in meiner Haut*), and so very much the aristocrat, that if they had made me a prince it would not have surprised me." I may say in passing that it would have become him to be a prince. Had he taken up Napoleon's invitation to transfer his activity to Paris, had he written there the *Cæsar* Napoleon wanted him to write, in which he need only have given vent to the hatred he had felt as a youth for the " base, the contemptible murder," the Emperor would certainly have made him a prince, as by his own account he would have done for Corneille as well. My point is to show how, in Goethe's mind, the consciousness of his social position lay very close to that of his nobility as a human being, as a child of God. The two flow together in one and the same consciousness of nobility, or " inborn merit."

Count Leo Tolstoy came, as we know, from one of the oldest and finest of Russian families. When we read his books, *Childhood, Boyhood, Youth,* or *Anna Karenine,* that picture of high life in Moscow, we are impressed with the fact that the author is a man who was brought up with all the advantages. We get the same feeling when we read *Dichtung und Wahrheit* or *Die Wahlverwandtschaften*. And in Tolstoy too we find the same familiar and perhaps childish phenomenon we noticed in Goethe: his noble blood and the distinction conferred by his great gifts both belonged to him quite simply because they belonged to him, and his consciousness of them mingled in his joy in himself, of which, despite all his attacks of poverty of spirit, he possessed a very great deal. His fame as a writer, so he wrote to his father-in-law, delights him very much; he finds it most pleasant to be an author *and* a nobleman. An author and a nobleman — all his Christianity, all his anarchism, to the contrary and notwithstanding, he never ceased to be a striking combination of those two. When Turgeniev first made the acquaintance of the youthful Tolstoy he said: "Not a word, not a gesture of his is natural. He is constantly posing; it is a mystery to me how such a sensible man can take such childish pride in his silly title." This is the same Turgeniev who wrote to a French publisher: "I am not worthy to untie his shoe-laces"; so it is unlikely that the first-quoted remark misrepresents the facts. As for the aged Tolstoy, Gorky relates: "His comfortable, democratic manner took many people in; and I have often seen Russians, who judge people by their clothes, gush over him with their famous 'simplicity of manner,' which might better be called 'beastly familiarity.' And suddenly, from under his peasant beard, and his rumpled democratic blouse, the old Russian *Barin,* the aristocrat of aristocrats, would peep forth; and in the chill that emanated from him the confiding visitor's nose would be frost-bitten. It was a joy to see this blue-blooded creature: the noble charm of his gestures, the haughty reticence of his speech, the murderous and fastidious sharpness of his tongue. He displayed just so much of the *Barin* as these servile souls needed to see; when they roused the *Barin* in Tolstoy it came easy and natural and overwhelmed them so that they shrivelled up and whined." — The blue noses call up memories of Weimar, chilling memories of receptions and formal calls — only that Goethe was never malicious enough to put on the democratic pose; and his most frigid manner concealed more love than Tolstoy ever felt — Tolstoy, whose last and most frightful secret Turgeniev's penetrating mind laid bare: it was that Tolstoy could love nobody but himself! But it was a " joy," in Gorky's sense of the word, to see Tolstoy for instance at the Petrov yearly fair, whither he drove from his estate in Samara in the seventies. His charm made him very popular in the merry whirl of peasants, Cossacks, Bashkirs, and Kirghiz. Even with drunken folk, we are told, he did not hesitate to strike up a conversation. And then came the following quiet and characteristic little episode. A drunken peasant, in his excess of feeling, wanted to embrace Tolstoy. But one stern and expressive look from Leo Nikolaevich's eyes met the man and sobered him in a twinkling. He dropped his hands of himself, and said: " No? Well, all right, then." What was there in that look to make it have such an arresting, quenching, sobering effect? Was it the consciousness of the *Barin?* Or of the great author? In such a case it is quite impossible to distinguish between them — as little objectively as doubtless it was subjectively.

"When Leo Nikolaevich wanted to please," Gorky tells us, "he could do it better than a pretty and clever woman. Imagine a crowd of all sorts of people sitting in his room: the Grand Duke Nicholai Michailovich, the house-painter Ilya, a social-democrat from Jalta, a musician, a German, the poet Bulgakov, and so on; they all look at him with the same enamoured eyes, while he expounds to them the doctrine of Lao Tse. . . . I used to look at him just like the others. And now I long to look at him once more — and I shall never see him again." — One thing is obvious: it was *not* the doctrine of Lao Tse which brought that lovelorn look into all their eyes. The teaching would have roused very scant general interest but for the expounder. But that look in every eye is the very same that Karl August had in mind when he passed on to Goethe the greetings sent by Napoleon on the Emperor's way back from Russia: "You see," he added, "heaven and hell are both making eyes at you."

Yes, and the democratic moujik blouses were immaculate, made of soft fine material, highly comfortable and pleasant to wear, and the linen was scented. Of course, he did not scent it himself. The Countess attended to that, and he, who liked it very much, pretended not to notice, just as he pretended not to know that the vegetarian dishes he exclusively ate were all prepared with *bouillon*. "His face is that of a peasant," reports an eyewitness, "with a broad nose, a weather-beaten skin, and thick, beetling brows with

61

small, piercing grey eyes beneath them. But, despite the peasant features, no one could fail to recognize at first glance the fine, cosmopolitan Russian gentleman, member of the very highest society." Conversing thus in English or French with a Grand Duke, he reminds one very much of Goethe, on whom princes waited, and who thought it no derogation of his nobility, human or divine, to season it with a little knack for polite nothings. When Tolstoy visited Alexander Herz in London, his daughter, young Natalia Alexandrovna, begged to be present in a dark corner, that she might behold in the flesh the author of *Childhood, Boyhood, Youth*. With beating heart she awaited Tolstoy's appearance. She was bitterly disappointed to see a man dressed in the latest fashion, with good manners and a flow of speech, the subject-matter of which was exclusively the cock-fights and boxing-matches he had seen in London. " Not a word that came from his heart, not a word that could have corresponded to my expectations, did I hear during the single interview at which I was present."

Nothing of the sort is reported of Dostoyevsky or Schiller. Never did these by their worldliness disappoint the expectations of their audience. The sons of spirit make personally a spiritual impression, as the hopeful average man expects those to do who are soul-shakers. That lofty, pallid, suffering-saint and criminal look of Dostoyevsky corresponded to the idea the Russians got of the phenomenon of his genius, just as Schiller's mild, intrepid, fanatical, and equally ailing physiognomy, with open shirt-collar and flowing silk neckerchief, corresponded to the image which the German mind might have formed of its hero. Whereas on the other hand Goethe, if we accept Riemer's description of him as he moved among his guests in a blue coat, " the powerful, expressive face showing the effects of sun and fresh air, with the black side-locks floating about it, the black hair bound in a queue, was more like a well-to-do, comfortable farmer, or a much-visited staff-officer in mufti, than like a shrinking and sensitive poet." And it is true, *a priori*, that neither of those other two ever estranged ardent admiration by displaying a banal enthusiasm for cock-fighting and boxing. Whereas the sense of sport, the taste for bodily exercise, physical training, and physical enjoyment, played an essential rôle in Tolstoy's life as in Goethe's. We call these tastes gentlemanly and thus indicate the physical basis of the well-born-ness which is of this world. " One must see him," wrote Riemer about Goethe; " how strong and firm he stands on his feet, with what bodily agility and sure step he moves. Early gymnastic training, dancing, skating, riding, even coursing and racing, had given him this mobility and suppleness; he could never make a false step on the worst path or be in danger of slipping or falling; easily and swiftly he passed over smooth ice, narrow foot-paths and bridges, and rocky steeps. As a youth he climbed among chasms and shingle with his princely friend, mounted towering rocks and Alpine crags with the boldness of a chamois; and so throughout his fifty years of geological exploration no mountain has been too high for him, no shaft too deep nor passage too low, no cave labyrinthine enough.

63

The great interest which Leo Tolstoy took in his body showed itself negatively as well as positively. Negatively, in his Christian and ascetic grumblings at his beastly physical, in such utterances as that the body is a hindrance to the good man, and in such phrases as: " I am ashamed to speak of my disgusting body." Positively, in all the training and care he gave it. His interest in it begins at the moment — of which he speaks in the *Confessions* — when he sat as a little child in a wooden tub, enveloped in the smell of the bran-water in which he was being bathed, and for the first time noticed his little body with the ribs visible on the breast in front, and straightway feels drawn to it by a very strong inclination. Tolstoy's face was, humanly speaking, ugly, and he suffered greatly on account of it, convinced that there could be little joy in store for a creature with such a broad nose, such thick lips, and such small grey eyes. He confesses that he would have given anything he had for a handsome face. The youth who is tortured by the problem of death, and ponders all the high and ultimate questions with as much maturity as the aged prophet, this youth is at the same time perpetually occupied with his own appearance, is obviously possessed by the desire to be elegant and *comme il faut;* sets the greatest store by physical development, gymnastic exercise; drills, rides, and hunts as though he had no higher ambition in his head nor thought of any. His passion for the hunt is so excessive that he confesses to his wife that of human beings he never forgot Sophia Alexandrovna, but out hunting he forgot everything but his double-barrelled shot-gun. From more than one letter of those who knew him in his prime we see what a daring sportsman he was, how he sprang with astonishing agility over gullies and chasms and would spend whole days in the wild. We are told that a better companion could not be conceived of. The pacifism, Christian, Buddhistic, or Chinese, of his latter days forbade him of course to kill animals, although his indestructible physical strength and trained agility would still have allowed him to hunt and though he still cherished the greatest desire to. He bade it farewell. He submitted himself to a test and found he had fortitude enough to let the hares run. And in his case that meant a good deal, as we see from the following anecdote, related by Gorky. Tolstoy put on a heavy overcoat and thick boots and took Gorky for a walk in the birch-woods. He leaped like a schoolboy over puddles and ditches, shook the rain-drops from the boughs, lovingly stroked the moist, satiny trunks of the birch-trees, and talked about Schopenhauer. . . . " Suddenly a hare got up under our feet. Leo Nikolaevich gave an excited start, his face lighted up, he let out a halloo like an old huntsman. Then he looked at me with a curious smile and began laughing, a hearty human laugh. At this moment he was irresistible." — Still finer is the story of the hawk which the old man saw circling above his chickens, about to swoop. Leo Nikolaevich stares up at the bird of prey, his hand over his eyes, and says in an " excited whisper ": " The rascal! Now, now! He's coming . . . oh, he's afraid. . . . I'll call the stable-boy." He calls, the hawk disappears. But Tolstoy is taken with regrets. He sighs and says: " I shouldn't have

65

called. Then he would have swooped." They are his chickens. But all the sympathy of the venerable prophet of pacifism is with the hawk.

Of his son Iliuscha he wrote in a letter: " Iliuscha is lazy, he is growing, and his soul is not yet overwhelmed by organic processes." What does he mean by that? Growing is itself an organic process, and if growing is innocent, so too will be the organic processes which growth brings about, and with which Tolstoy was only too well acquainted, since they made his life a burden to him all his days. The Church's conception of woman as *instrumentum diaboli* was with him something more than a mood from the time of the *Kreuzer Sonata*; it dates from much earlier, from the journals of his boyish days; and he speaks of organic processes in the sense of that early Christian pope who, in order to mortify the flesh, made a detailed list of all its disgusting and evil-smelling functions, the functions of this body which in the end has to submit to the final indignity of putrefaction. That kind of cross-grained speculation Tolstoy would be just the one to set about, and he did. Very sensual men well know such moods. Maupassant somewhere calls the act of coition filthy and ridiculous — " *ordurier et ridicule.*" Could objectivity further go? But such blithe and cynical objectivity was not Tolstoy's sort. His hatred of the organic has a shattering accent of subjective torment and rage. And yet he is so much the darling of the creative impulse of organic life that one must go back to Goethe to find a human being who was " *so wohl in seiner Haut* " as he. Yes, the parallel is even more exact. In both of them, and in just

66

the same way, the most beatific organic well-being, amounting to organic rapture, mingled with a rooted melancholy and the profoundest intimacy with death. Goethe, when he was a riotous, dandiacal student in Leipsic, might any moment quit the society of men, the card-play and dance, and yield himself to solitude. We have plenty of witnesses to his brilliance, his childish, fantastic extravagances in the circle of his friends, with the Jacobis, Heinse, Stilling in Elberfeld. He cuts capers, dances round the table like a clown, in short cannot contain himself for a mysterious intoxication; the philistines sitting round think he has gone mad. And that is the same Goethe whose Werther drove more than one young man to self-destruction, and who practised himself in suicide by keeping a sharp dagger on his bed-table and trying every evening to drive it a little further into his body.

We have noted the same excess of animal spirits in Tolstoy; in whom, indeed, they persisted up to an old age lacking in the dignity, stateliness, and formal gravity of Goethe's latest period. Which need surprise nobody. For we cannot doubt that Goethe led a more earnest, laborious, exemplary life than the Slavic junker; or that his cultural activities presupposed far more genuine self-abnegation, restraint, and discipline than Tolstoy's uttermost ineffectual efforts at spiritualization, sticking fast as these always did in a bog of fantastic absurdity. Tolstoy's aristocratic charm was, and Gorky so depicts it, that of a noble animal. He never managed to arrive at the dignity of man the civilized, man the triumpher over odds. It is lovely to hear of all the pranks he played with the children, his droll conceits, the gymnastic feats he performed for and with them; the endless croquet, lawn-tennis, and leap-frog parties in the garden at Yasnaya Polyana. He not only shared all the activities of youth, but he was the life and soul of them. The sixty-year-old man runs races with the boys, his bicycle trips extend, much to the Countess's anxiety, over thirty versts. " When there is some activity requiring agility, strength, and suppleness," comments a bystander, " he never takes his eyes off the players, he puts his whole soul into their success or failure. Often he cannot resist and joins in with a youthful fire and muscular flexibility which the onlooker could only envy." In the family circle he performed the sheerest absurdities. He had invented a game called Numidian Horsemen, which made the children weep with delight. Leo Nikolaevich would suddenly spring from his chair, lifting his hand, and run about the room flapping it in the air, whereupon everybody, grown-ups, children, and all, followed suit. That is, I repeat, charming, though a little bizarre. It becomes more so when we learn that all these high spirits occur in the years after his " conversion," in the period of his soul-crises, his ascetic eclipses and theological broodings. But what shall be said of the incident recorded by his father-in-law, Behrs? They were walking about the room together in light converse, one evening, when suddenly the elderly prophet sprang upon Behrs's shoulder. He probably jumped down again at once; but for a second he actually perched up there, like a grey-bearded kobold —

68

it gives one an uncanny feeling! I do not ask my readers to imagine Goethe, in his later period, leaping unexpectedly on a visitor's shoulder. There is a decided difference of temperament, that is clear. But the resemblance is no less so.

Looking more closely at the matter, I find that there is a complex of problems, a " problematic," peculiar to the sons of nature, the creative and objective artists, which is entirely foreign to the children of the idea, and, for all the brilliant sunshine of favour they move in, casts a strange dark cloud upon them which must considerably chill their consciousness of aristocratic well-being. My feeling is that it is pure error to think that conflict and complexity are things of the spirit, while nature's kingdom must be all brightness and harmony. It looks as though the contrary were the case. If what we call happiness consists in harmony, clarity, unity with oneself, in the consciousness of a positive, confident, decisive turn of mind, if, in short, it is peace resident in the soul, then obviously happiness is a state far easier for the sons of spirit to arrive at than for the children of nature. For the latter, though surely singleness of heart should be their lot, seem never to attain the joy and peace it might confer. Nature herself appears to weave in their very being a questionable strand, an element of contradiction, negation, and all-pervasive doubt, which, since it cannot conduce to goodness, cannot conduce to happiness either. Spirit is good. Nature is by no means good. One might say she is evil, if moral categories were admissible with reference to her. She is, then, neither good nor evil, she escapes definition, as she herself refuses to define and judge; she is, speaking objectively, indifferent, and as this indifference of hers appears subjectively and spiritually in her children, it becomes a complication that has more to do with torment and evil than with happiness and goodness, and which certainly seems come not to bring peace into the world, like the human and benevolent spirit, but rather doubt and dire confusion.

Obviously I am not speaking here of the comparatively harmless conflict between the Faustian " two souls," the battle between the impulses of a strong animal constitution and the yearnings after *" Gefilden hoher Ahnen "* — a battle, and a " problematic," of which Goethe speaks out of such deep experience, and which not only made Tolstoy's youth a period of such hardship, so torn with remorse, but persisted in him up to old age. I am speaking of something which seems at first blush to be much blither and simpler: a position something like that of Goethe between Lavater and Basedow, in which Goethe designates himself as *" das Weltkind in der Mitten."* That sounds simple, and pleasant, and self-complacent, and was probably so meant. And yet in the word *" Weltkind "* and the associations that surround it there is something sinister, a difficulty and a " problematic," by contrast with which the " prophetic " existence is nothing less than sweetness and light and plain sailing. " Goethe's tendency to negation," writes Chancellor von Müller on some occasion or other, " and his incredible judicial-mindedness came out strong again."

" There is something," Gorky writes about Tolstoy, " which presumably he will never reveal to a human being, which appears darkly in his conversation, and is hinted at in his journals. To me it seems like the apotheosis of negation, the deepest and most hideous nihilism, springing from a stratum of boundless and hopeless despair, from a solitude of which probably no one else in the world has ever been so frightfully aware." No one? It was not Tolstoy who created the so lyric figure of Mephistopheles — though indeed the Mephistophelian element was never lacking to any period of his life. The ceaseless, tormenting effort to shape that which he calls his conception of life, to arrive at truth and clarity and inward peace, found expression in his youth, partly in a gloomy irritability that led to duels and scenes with his friends, which he took in desperate earnest, as matters of life and death, killing and dying; but partly also in malicious negation in general, an inimical spirit of contradictiousness, which, as we are expressly assured, made a quite Mephistophelian impression. Though of course this was not a nihilistic but a moral attitude, and was not assumed save in opposition to things that were not true — only they were simply everything! In the young Tolstoy there was observable, " from the beginning, a sort of unconscious enmity toward all accepted laws in the kingdom of thought. No matter what the opinion expressed; and the greater the authority of the speaker, the more was Tolstoy at pains to take up and accentuate an inimical attitude. If you watched him as he listened, and saw the sarcastic curl of his lip, you could not avoid the impression that he was thinking, not so much of answering what was said, as of himself saying something which should surprise and confound the speaker." That is nihilism, that is malice. But it is not so much cold malice as it is a tortured spite against anybody who fancied he held the secret of clarity and truth. It is a disbelief in clarity and truth. This spite, and this incredulity, were especially directed against Turgeniev, the clear-eyed and human man with whom he never could get on. " Tolstoy," said Turgeniev, " early developed a trait which, lying as it does at the root of his gloomy conception of life, has caused him great suffering. He has never managed to believe in the sincerity of mankind. Every expression of feeling seemed to him false; and he had the habit, due to his extraordinarily penetrating gaze, of boring through with his eye the man he considered insincere." And when Turgeniev said this, he added the confession that never in his life had he encountered anything with such power to dishearten him as this same piercing gaze, which, accompanied by two or three biting remarks, could bring to the verge of madness anybody who did not possess particularly strong self-control. Now Turgeniev's self-control was strong. He was at the height of his literary success; serene and untroubled, he could encounter the complexities of his younger colleague with the calmness of a man who lived on good terms with himself. But precisely this security was what troubled Tolstoy. He seems to have gone deliberately about with this tranquil, good-natured man, working with such a clear conviction that what he did was right, to goad him past the bounds of self-control.

Simply this conviction that he knew and did what was right was more than Tolstoy could bear; for certainly he himself did not in the least know what was right. Garschin says: "In his view, the people who passed for good were merely hypocrites, who paraded their goodness and pretended to the certainty that their work served a good end." Turgeniev too saw in Tolstoy this strange, sinister, malicious bent. He resolved to hold fast to what he considered "right" and not to lose his self-control; so he avoided Tolstoy, left Saint Petersburg, where the latter was living, and went first to Moscow and then to his own estate. But — this is most significant of all, as evidence of Tolstoy's state of mind —Tolstoy followed him. Followed him step for step, "like a lovesick girl," to use Turgeniev's own phrase.

All which is very telling, very extraordinary. Above all, it shows how completely the old Tolstoy, of whom Gorky writes, was foreshadowed in the young one. Did he really ever find out what was "right" — the real, the true, the incontrovertible? For others he did, he gave them conviction. But he himself certainly never got free of the negation and neutrality of the elemental character. "Rousseau," he said, "lied and believed his lies." Did he believe his own lies? No, for he did not lie. He was elemental, nihilistic, malicious, and unfathomable. "Would you very much like to know?" he asks. — "Very much." — "Then I will not tell you." And he smiles and plays with his thumbs. This smile, this "sly little smile" — Gorky speaks of it again and again. There is something not only extra-moral but extra-mental, extra-human, about it; it bespeaks the mystery of the "natural," the elemental, which is not at all kindly disposed, but rather takes pleasure in confusion. According to Gorky, the old man loved to put insidious questions. "What do you think about yourself?" "Do you love your wife?" "How do you like mine?" "Do you like me, Alexei Maximovich?" — "Disingenuous!" Gorky cries. "The whole time, he is making an experiment, testing something out, as though he were going into battle. It is interesting, but not to my taste. He is the devil, and I am a babe in arms beside him. He ought to leave me alone."

One day Gorky sees the aged Tolstoy sitting alone by the sea. This scene is the crowning point of his reminiscences. "He sat, his head on his hands; the wind blew the silver hair of his beard through his fingers. He was looking far out across the sea, and the little green waves rolled docilely to his feet and caressed them, as though they wanted to tell the old wizard something about themselves. . . . He seemed like an ancient stone come alive, that knew and pondered the beginning and end of all things, and what and how would be the end of the stones and grasses of the earth, the waters of the sea, the whole universe from the sun to the grain of sand. And the sea is a part of his soul, and all about him comes from him and out of him. In the old man's musing quietude I felt something portentous, magic. I cannot express in words what I more felt than thought at that moment. In my heart were rejoicing and fear, then all melted together in one single blissful feeling: ' I am not bereft on this earth, so long as this old man is living on it.' " And Gorky steals away on his tiptoes that the sand may not crunch under his tread and disturb the old man's thoughts.

The mystical reverence that Gorky here depicts is not that which lays hold on us at sight of the heroes of the idea. Neither Dostoyevsky nor Schiller has inspired this sort of awe and shuddering, however saintly they seemed. So much is certain. Nor can the reverence felt for Goethe be of just this same nature — though akin to it. The Tolstoyan greatness and remoteness is wild and primeval and pagan in its nature, it is antecedent to culture. It lacks the human, the humanistic element. This ancient of days and of wisdom, musing there at the edge of the everlasting sea, wrapped up in the All, conning the beginning and end of things — the picture evokes a twilit, prehuman, uncanny world of feeling, a world of incantations and runes. What he is pondering, the norns whisper thee by night. He was like, says the shaken beholder, an ancient stone come alive: note that, a stone, not anything that civilization has produced, not man made in the likeness of God, not a human being like Goethe. Goethe's humanistic divineness is clearly something quite different from the primeval, pagan formlessness of Tolstoy's, which makes Gorky say of him: " He is the devil." And still, at the very bottom, the common factor persists: in Goethe too there is the elemental, the sinister, the dark, neutral, negation- and confusion-loving devil.

There is a saying of his, arbitrary enough, yet with an accent of hidden suffering, that opens to us more of his

inner self than many a clear and wise and ordered utterance. " If I am to listen to the opinion of others," he said
(and only listen to it, observe, not accept it), " then it must
be positively expressed. Problems I have enough in myself." That is a confession, put in the form of a demand. It
has a proud, Olympian accent, but the voice that utters
it quivers with impatience, with painful irritation at the
inner complications, which makes it so imperative that the
positive should come from without. . . . " Out of one of
his eyes looks an angel," writes someone who made his
acquaintance on a journey, " out of the other a devil; and
his speech is deep irony on the score of all human affairs."
Of all? That is great, but it is not generous — and, after
all, is he not a man himself? One who often saw him says:
" Today he was altogether in that mood of bitter humour
and sophistical contradictiousness he is so prone to display." Again we have the negation, the spirit of contradiction and malice, of which gentle young Sulpice Boisserée has such a story to tell in his diary. " At eleven o'clock
I am with Goethe again. The invective continues." He has a
go at all sorts of things: politics, æsthetics, society, religion,
Germany, France, philhellenism, parties, and so on,
in such a style that poor young Boisserée feels — " *mit
allen diesen moquanten Reden* " — as though he were " at
a witches' sabbath." That is saying a good deal. It is either
too strong, considering the word " *moquant* " which he
uses, or else that word is a good deal too weak — which is
more likely. Anyhow the entry, from the year 1826, shows
the confusion to which the petulant old man could reduce

simple and humble-minded people. An observer who must have been no fool wrote something about him which stirs a secret horror that is somehow paralysing. " He is tolerant, without being mild." Just consider what that means. Toleration, indulgence, is always, in our human experience, associated with mildness, with benevolent feeling toward man and the universe; so far as I know, it is a product of love. But tolerance *without* love, *harsh* tolerance — what would that be? It is more than human, it is icy neutrality, it is either something godlike or something devilish.

I shall be saying nothing new, but it may serve to bring order and clarity into our thoughts to keep the fact before us: all national character belongs to the natural sphere, and all tendency toward the cosmopolitan to the spiritual. The word " ethnic " brings together two conceptions which we do not ordinarily connect, paganism and nationalism; thus by implication, and conversely, every super-national and humane point of view is classified in our mind as Christian in spirit.

Goethe's alleged devotion to paganism (in the *Wanderjahre* he reckons Judaism among the ethnic and heathen folk-religions) would lead us accordingly to expect of him an outlook basically anti-humanistic and folk-national. That we should be entirely wrong in this expectation, as a basic constitution in him, as " nature," might be arguable. However, so far as he was himself aware, he was consciously a humanist and a citizen of the world. Despite all his nature Olympian and divine, he was in a high degree Christian in spirit. Nietzsche placed Goethe, historically and psychologically speaking, between Hellenism and pietism; and thus expressed the combination of creative and critical, simple and "sentimental," ancient and modern, in Goethe's character. For Goethe's "pietism" is of course nothing else than his modernity. Many centuries of Christian cultivation of the subjective — a whole century of pietistic, introspective, autobiographical discipline — were needed to make possible a work like *Werther*. Which is as much as to say that in the impulse to autobiography Christian and democratic elements are mingled with that naïve, spoilt-darling claim on the world's affections of which we spoke above. They are the same as that democratic tendency out of which Tolstoy likes to consider his confessions as emanating; when, in true Rousseauian fashion, he resolves " to write a history of his life, utterly and entirely true to fact," in the belief that this " will be more useful to mankind " than those previous twelve volumes full of literary twaddle. He seems unaware that they are quite as autobiographical, quite as ethical in character, as anything could be, and disowns them as pagan and artistic, as self-indulgent and " irresponsible."

Goethe, with all his aversion to the " Cross," did often and expressly acknowledge his reverence for the Christian idea. It is as significant as it is surprising to come upon the idea of the sanctity of suffering in the Pedagogic Province; and if Goethe saw in the Church " elements of weakness and instability " and in its precepts " *gar viel Dummes*," still he bore witness that " there is in the Gospels an effective resplendence and majesty, issuing from the person of Christ, of a character in which only the divine appear upon this earth." " The human spirit," he says, with sympathetic and openly acknowledged fellowship, " will never rise higher than the majesty and moral elevation of Christianity, as it radiates from the Gospels." But Goethe's Christianity manifests itself in the admirable attitude, as of a pupil to a master, which he had toward Spinoza, whom he called " *theissimus* " and of whom he said that nobody had spoken of the Divinity so like the Saviour as he. If, indeed, the dualistic separation of God and nature is the fundamental principle of Christianity, then Spinoza was a pagan, and Goethe was too. But God and nature are not all the world: there is the human, the humane, as well; and Spinoza's conception of humanity is Christian, in so far as he defines the phenomenon man as the becoming-*conscious* of the God-nature in the human being, as a bursting forth out of mere dull being and living; accordingly, as liberation from nature, and so as *spirit*. Again, there is absolutely nothing pagan about that famous *Mastery of the Passions by their Analysis;* and just as little in the Spinozan motif of renunciation ("*Entsagung*"), which becomes the general motif of Goethe's life and work, like the idea of freedom for Schiller and the idea of redemption for Wagner.

On the contrary, it was just this pathos of renunciation, which cast such a Christian shade upon the pagan, aristocratic, child-of-nature well-being of Goethe's life and lent his spirited features an expressly Gothic trait of

suffering not to be overlooked save by the gross popular belief in his aristocratic good fortune. How much resignation
must have darkened the end of this apparently consummate and favoured existence! His life-work, though almost
superhuman, remained entirely a fragment — it is putting
it mildly to say that "not all the dreams of blossoms
ripened" — Wagner's performance, for instance, or
Ibsen's, is incomparably more a rounded and effective
whole. One may put it that Goethe's spirit was far more
powerful than his nature, greater than his power to give
it form or than his organically allotted span; and it is
easy to understand that vehement demand of his for immortality, which is one of the magnificent, dæmonic expressions of his personality: Nature, he cried, was bound
to give him a new body when the one he had could no longer
sustain his spirit.

Consider even his love-life, which likewise the popular
mind tends to think of as sunlit and blissful, divinely favoured and without a cross. Certainly he was much loved
and rich in love; certainly to him much enjoyment was
given. In the realm of the erotic he had his spells of coarse-
ness, when he behaved a little like a garden god: when,
ingenuous and unsentimental as the antique world, he
would enjoy without stint and indulge without a qualm.
His marriage, a misalliance, socially and intellectually,
was a result of this attitude of mind. But where he loved
so that lofty poesy was the result, and not merely a Vene-
tian epigram ticked out in hexameters on a maiden's back;
where it was serious, the romance regularly ended in re-

nunciation. He never actually possessed Lotte or Frie-
derike, nor Lilli, nor the Herzlieb, nor Marianne, nor even
Ulrike — and not even Frau von Stein. He never loved
unrequited — unless in the immensely painful, absurdly
agitating affair with little Levetzof. Yet in all these cases
resignation was the order of the day: either on moral
grounds, or for the sake of his freedom. Mostly he bolted.

But the renunciation I mean was a deeper and higher
thing. In his stature, his lineaments, his proportions as he
stands today in the eyes of the nation, he is what he is as
the work of renunciation. I am not speaking generally, I
do not refer to the sense of sacrifice which is the meaning
of all art; nor to the struggle with chaos, the surrender
of freedom, the creative constraint which is its inner essence. Goethe's pathos of renunciation — or, since we are
speaking of permanent forces dominating the whole of
existence, his ethos of renunciation — is of a more personal kind. It is his destiny, it is the instinctive mandate of
his especially national gift, which was essentially civilizing in its mission. Or, rather, might this destiny and mission,
this bond, this conditioning limitation and pedagogic duty
of renunciation, be after all something less personal to
him than it just now appeared? Might it perhaps be the law
of his destiny, innate and inviolable save at the expense
of heavy spiritual penalties; the imperative which is the
essence of the German spirit, destined always, as it is,
somehow and in some degree, to feel itself called to a
cultural task? — I spoke of the consciousness of a community of feeling, which Goethe must, at moments, have

felt with Christianity. What did it consist in, and to what had it reference? Goethe pays homage to the " moral culture" of Christianity — that is, to its humanity, its civilizing, anti-barbarian influence. It was the same as his; and the occasional homage he paid it undoubtedly springs from his recognition that the mission of Christianity within the confines of the Germanic peoples bore a likeness to his own. And here, in the fact that he conceived his task, his duty to his nation, as essentially a civilizing mission, lies the deepest and the most German significance of his renunciation. Does anyone doubt that there were in Goethe possibilities of a greatness and growth, wilder, ranker, more disruptive, more " natural," than those which his instinct for self-conquest allowed him to develop, and which today give our mental picture of him so highly pedagogic a cast? In his *Iphigenia* the idea of humanity, as opposed to barbarism, wears the impress of civilization — not in the polemical and even political sense in which we use the word today, but in the sense of moral culture. It was a Frenchman, Maurice Barrès, who pointed out that the *Iphigenia* is a " civilizing work," in that it " stands for the rights of society against the arrogance of intellect." The phrase fits almost better that other monument of self-discipline and self-correction, yes, almost of self-mortification, which has been a target for ridicule on account of its affected atmosphere of courts and culture: I mean the *Tasso*. Both are works of resignation, of German and schoolmasterish renunciation of all the advantages of barbarism. Wagner, on the other hand, the voluptuary, did not renounce them; he yielded to them all, with huge effectiveness; and his punishment is that the acclaim accorded to his riotously national art grows daily cruder and more popular.

My subject is still the aspiration of the children of nature toward spirit; which is just as sentimental in kind as is the converse striving of the sons of the spirit toward nature, and may function with varying degrees of aptitude or success, with more or less naïveté or subtlety. Compared with Goethe's majestic work of spiritualization, I cannot find that Tolstoy's struggles to throw off nature's yoke were crowned with great success. But I am whimsical enough to relish putting my finger on the mighty kernel of racial loyalty which dwelt at the heart of the Christianity of the one and the humanity of the other. And that kernel was, of course, in other words, their aristocratic integrity; for racial loyalty is aristocratic by nature, while Christianity, humanity, and civilization all represent the conflicting principle of the spirit of democracy, and the process of spiritualization is at the same time one of democratization. What Tolstoy aptly calls his " democratic trend " — aptly, because the word " trend " implies a will and a direction somewhither, indicating an effort and not mere being — finds emphatic expression now and again in Goethe as well. " One would have," he says, "to become *Catholic* at once, in order to have a share in the lives of humanity! " To mingle with humanity, on equal terms, to lead the life of the people, and in the market-place, seems at such moments happiness to him. " In these small sovereign states," he cries, " what wretched, isolated men we are!" And he praises Venice as a monument to the power, not of a single despot, but of a whole people. But such phrases, clearly, are meant more correctively than absolutely; they are self-critical comments, meant to redress the balance of his German and Protestant aristocratism — "tendencies," then, sentimental leanings, of the same kind as the radical and pacifistic bent of the Russian giant, in whose "holiness" a penetrating eye can see so much self-deception, childishness, and "let's pretend."

A close observer like Gorky, or a shrewd critic like Merezhkovsky, felt at once and keenly the patriarchal and sensual quality, the life-bound animalism, which lay beneath the sanctification. Tolstoy married at thirty-four the eighteen-year-old Sophia Alexandrovna Behrs, who from then on was scarcely ever anything but "expectant," and was confined thirteen times. Through long, creative years, his marriage was an idyll of family life, full of healthy, god-fearing animal pleasure, against a lavish economic background of agriculture and cattle-breeding. The atmosphere was Judaic Old Testament rather than Christian. Tolstoy knows the same great simple love of existence, the everlasting childlike joy of life, that possessed Goethe's soul. When he "praises each day for its beauty," when he "marvels at the richness of God's kingdom" expressing itself therein, how "each day He sends some new thing to distinguish it," we feel a better understanding of what lay at the bottom of Goethe's conception of "*Behagen*." Waves of piercing sensuous enjoyment of nature break upon him even in the years of gloom, when he meditates suicide, plans the *Confession* — in short, conjures up that misunderstanding to which his sanctification falls prey, and dehumanizes and shrinks the majesty of the patriarch, christianizes and conventionalizes it into the Anglo-Indian model.

Merezhkovsky called him the great seer of the body, in contrast to Dostoyevsky the visionary of the soul; and truly it is the body to which his love and deepest interest belong, to which his knowledge refers, by which his genius is conditioned. We see this so clearly in his reaction to old age. In 1894 he writes: " Age is approaching. That means the hair falls out, the teeth decay, the wrinkles come, the breath gets bad. Even before the end, everything turns frightful, disgusting; sweat, rouge, powder, all sorts of beastliness. Then what has become of that which I have served? Where has beauty gone? It is the essence of everything. Without it there is nothing, no life." — This description of dying while the body still lives, may pass for Christian, by virtue of its insistence on misery and its characterization of the flesh, revolting and insulting on the spiritual side. But the physical apprehension of old age and death is through and through pagan and sensual.

Aksakov says of Tolstoy: "His gift is *bearlike* in kind and degree." And is it not this " bearlike " quality of his genius that made Tolstoy " the great writer of Russia," the author of *War and Peace,* the epic poet of the people's struggle against Rome, against Napoleon? I openly declare my deliberate intention to cast doubt on the pacifism which the prophet of humanity so didactically professed. Not,

I hasten to add, from any anti-pacifistic sentiments on my own part; merely out of a sense of humour. That Tolstoy was in his youth a soldier and an officer, we know. From his biography we learn that he was heart and soul a soldier; and we have evidence of his heroic and warlike enthusiasm in the Sebastopol days — that " splendid time," that "glorious time," that time of touching pride in the Russian army, when he was confessedly saturated with patriotic feeling and thrilled by his experience of comradery under arms, first felt when the serious moment is at hand. His attitude toward the Serbo-Turkish war of 1877 is still full of conviction. It is a *real* war, he says, and it moves him. The distinction between " real " and " unreal " doubtless indicates some progress in the direction of pacifism. But is pacifism " real " so long as it is conditional and must progress in order to exist?

In 1812, at least, there *was* a " real " war, and its history occupied Tolstoy long before he became the great writer of Russia by dint of it. He treated of it, quite in the patriotic key, in his school at Yasnaya Polyana. From all we hear, he dealt with it on a mythical rather than a historical basis; but he expressly declared that he presented his pupils with these legends of a warlike mythology in order to rouse their patriotic feeling. And then the root-and-branch Russianism, the fundamental folk-character of his peasant-patrician nature, comes out strong in his epos, whose theme is a defensive war waged against the invasion of Latin civilization. *War and Peace* had a huge popular success, though the critics and military men had some fault to find. *On the intellectual side it was weak,* they said; its philosophy of history was narrow and superficial; it was mysticism and sophistry to deny the influence of individuals on events. But the creative power, the "bear-like" strength of it, were unanimously declared to be beyond all discussion, as well as its enormous genuineness as a folk-epic. The liberal criticism of Russia admitted that it was "Russian to the core," that it "presented the soul of the Russian people, in its whole range and variety, in all its lofty simplicity, with a sheer creative power that had never been equalled." But the critics took in bad part Tolstoy's "wilful remoteness from all contemporary *currents of progress*" — a phenomenon and a reproach which were to recur with the appearance of *Anna Karenine.* "*Anna Karenine* I don't like," Turgeniev wrote, "though there are splendid things in it: the race, the mowing, the hunt. But the whole thing is soured; it *smells of Moscow,* and old maids and incense and Slavophils and high life and all that." In a word, Turgeniev, the *Sapadnik,* rejected with horror the oriental element in the novel, and with him went the whole liberal-radical party; some ignored *Anna Karenine,* others sneered or called names, while the Slavophils and the aristocrats and court party rubbed their hands in glee. In fact Tolstoy, in an intellectual and political sense, had the reactionaries on his side; and they could have little appreciation of the artistic qualities of his work. The liberals were liberal enough to know how to value these, and they did so, albeit in that state of bewilderment into which people always fall at the sight of genius in the camp of reaction. Witness the bewilderment of Europe over Bismarck.

The paradox is worth a little attention. Our idealists would have us believe that genius, the creative power, must, as a living force, act only in the service of progress and human purpose, and be justly denied to the forces which side against life, show sympathy with death, and are inimical to freedom and progress and thus bad in the human sense. We would almost accept it as metaphysical evidence for the goodness of a thing if a capital piece of writing were done in its name. And really, it does seem that, as a rule, the reactionary camp suffers from lack of talent. But not invariably. The reactionary genius does occur, the brilliant and conquering ability does act as attorney for retrograde tendencies — and nothing dazes the world more than the sight of this paradoxical phenomenon. Sainte-Beuve said of Joseph de Maistre that he had " nothing of a writer but the gift " — a comment which perfectly expresses this bewilderment and precisely indicates the thing I mean.

Liberal and progressive Russia must have seen in Tolstoy just this — a case of a great gift in the service of reaction. But it is clear enough that this great gift is of one essence with his fundamental Russianism, his immense integration with the people, his pagan and natural aristocracy; and that the tendency toward democratic spiritualization was — just tendency, romantic in its nature and crowned, after all, by such strikingly indifferent success! His tremendous orientalism found intellectual expression

88

in this mockery at and denial of European progress; and this it was which must necessarily and profoundly alienate all the westernizing and liberalizing, all the " Petrinic " elements in Russia. Actually, he quite frankly scouted the western belief in progress, which, he said, had been accepted by the Russia of Peter the Great. They had, he said, observed the operation of the law of progress in the Duchy of Hohenzollern-Sigmaringen, with its three thousand inhabitants. But then came China, with its two hundred million inhabitants, and knocked the theory of progress into a cocked hat. Which did not for one moment prevent them from believing in progress as a general law of mankind; they took the field with cannons and guns to instruct the Chinese in their thesis. Yet ordinary human understanding tells us that if the history of the larger part of mankind, which we call the Orient, does not confirm the law of progress, then this law does not obtain for the whole of mankind, but forms at most an article of faith for a certain part of it. Tolstoy vows that he himself is unable to find a universal law in the life of mankind, and that history might be co-ordinated just as well in the light of any other idea or " historical whimsy " as in that of progress. And more than that, he does not see the slightest necessity of finding laws for history — quite apart from the impossibility of the thing. The universal, eternal law of perfection, he says, stands written in the soul of every human being; it is only an error to carry it over into the field of history. So long as it remains personal, this law is fruitful and accessible to all; applied to historical conceptions, it is idle talk. The

89

general progress of mankind is an unproved thesis. It does not exist for any of the nations of the east; hence it is just as unfounded to assert that progress is a primary law of mankind as it would be to say that blondness is — all people being blond save those with dark hair.

It is remarkable to see how ideas from the sphere of an idealistic individualism, which is German, and places human perfection within the individual soul, are here found in the company of others which constitute the most decisive challenge to an arrogant Europe setting itself up as intellectual arbiter of the world. Tolstoy protests against what he considers the childishness of this attitude, which confuses western Europe with humanity as a whole; and the protest betrays that his gaze is directed eastward. It betrays, in a word, his Asiatic bias: anti-"Petrinic," primitive Russian, anti-civilization — in short, *bearlike*. What we hear is the voice of the Russian god on the maple throne under the golden lime-tree.

The voice of our humanistic deity has a different ring. Goethe, beyond a doubt, hated and scorned Asia. The element of Sarmatian wildness in which Tolstoy found himself so much at home and which merely gets rationalized in his late prophetic period, would always remain remote and foreign to the spirit of the great German, with its exclusively cultural bias. A journey Goethe once made into Upper Silesian Poland was the occasion of what contact he had with the Slav. His impressions are " mostly remarkably negatively." He observes ignorance, lack of culture, low standards of living, stupidity. He feels himself " remote from cultured men." His attitude at the time of the War of Liberation, offensive as it was to patriotic feeling, the admiring and personally friendly respect he felt for the classic phenomenon of Napoleon (" the man is too big for you ") belong in this same category. " It is true," he says in 1813, " I no longer see French and Italians, but in their stead I see Cossacks, Bashkirs, Croats, Magyars, Kashubes, brown and other hussars." This enumeration of eastern races has an extraordinarily contemptuous ring. That the Cossacks and Kashubes were in the country as allies and the French as enemies seems not to matter to him. He confesses, indeed, that he too is glad to be rid of the Gallic *soldatesca*; yet he is obviously not far from finding more humiliation in the alliance with Russia and the dependence of Germany upon the east than in her subjugation upon the west; and certain it is that the humanism of the writer who created the *Iphigenia* has more affiliation with the humanity of western Europe, which has given the mould to our civilization, than with the soft and savage human nature of Half-Asia.

Unpatriotically he declared that he could not hate the French — he owed them far too much of his culture. The words are only right and proper. But (just as in Tolstoy's case) the fun begins directly it is a question of his nature, of that pre-intellectual fundamental constitution we were talking about, which had its own ways of finding expression, and which is so extraordinarily un-French that it might well be described as pre-eminently German. It would be wrong to bring in evidence here his coldness towards

" freedom." For in the first place the principle of order (*ordre*) is something just as French and classic and rationalist as the principle of freedom, which on party grounds is set over against it. And in the second, there is nothing un-German about freedom. We know with what éclat Goethe cited Guizot's dictum that Germany gave the idea of personal freedom to the world. But there is in Goethe something that rebels against the idea, against the doctrinaire and theoretic; a lack of faith that the particular, existing under definite conditions, could ever be improved by the method of abstraction; a realism, that is, and a scepticism, in matters political, which one may as well call un-French as particularly German — taking France as the country of revolution and Germany as the country of a certain national weakness for the living, historically conditioned, " organic." We must remember that he was a practical politician, he had governed Saxe-Weimar. But the practical sphere is not kind to the soul; it is a training in cynicism, as many a politician has found out, even in France, where more than one radical has become a conservative and turned the guns on the people after he came to power. Perhaps Goethe might have been more generous-minded, politically speaking, if he had not lost his idealism in the practical field. But this too is unlikely, since from the very beginning he was insensitive to historical democracy, to history defined as the evolution of the idea in the masses; he was fundamentally unacquainted with enthusiasm for political ideas, and in general conceived of history as the biography of great men — an aristocratism which is as different from

Schiller's high-flung democratic gesture as it is from the Christian-moujik disparagement of heroes in *War and Peace*.

It would be foolish to think of him as servile, despite the anecdote about Beethoven and the imperial company on the promenade at Karlsbad. His subservience to princes was purely mundane in its character, wherever no personal friendship came in play. When in 1794 Freiherr von Gagern published his challenge to the intelligence of Germany, and to Goethe in particular, to put its pen at the service of the " good," that is to say, the conservative cause — no other than that of a new alliance of German princes for the purpose of saving the country from anarchy — Goethe, after thanking him politely for the confidence reposed in him, made the characteristic reply that he considered it impossible for princes and writers to unite upon a common task. Notwithstanding which, we need waste no words over his strictly negative attitude toward the French Revolution.

On the intellectual side, his view of humanity was a cynical one — that is to say, it was radically sceptical. But we know that this was on the intellectual side alone, from the fact that it did not prevent him from loving his fellow-men. We have his confession that the mere sight of the human countenance could cure him of the blues. What he did not believe in was drawing up articles and holding love-feasts. We shall never know whether Hegel was mocking or spoke in honest enthusiasm when he said: " As long as the sun has stood in the firmament and the planets

93

circled round it, it has never been seen that a human being stands on his head — i.e., on his understanding — and bases reality upon it." Whether jest or earnest, it was this that revolted Goethe. He judged it to be entirely against nature to try to insist that the whole of mankind find just one choice of means, just one route toward civic happiness. Upon which I may comment as follows: that, in the first place, one such utterance, by virtue of its strongly nationalist, individualist, aristocratic emphasis, outweighs the whole burden of his indifference toward the War of Liberation, and that surely he who uttered it was only prevented by his admiration for the genius of Napoleon — likewise aristocratic in its origin — from seeing in the *Imperator* the standard-bearer of precisely this democratic "insistency." But, in the second place, we must admit that he had a right to set up as an advocate of nature. To quote again:

> *Franztum drängt in unsern verworrenen Tagen, wie einstmals*
>
> *Luthertum es getan, ruhige Bildung zurück.*
>
> (Driven by the spirit of France in our troublous days, as aforetime
>
> By the spirit of Luther oppressed, quiet culture retreats.)

What a telling synthesis this, of France and Luther; how unprejudiced by national feeling! It is all one to him whether the unrest, the distraction, come from this side or that of the Rhine. No matter whence it comes, it is his enemy, the enemy of nature and culture, of the *ruhige Bildung* which is at the bottom of his idea of humanity.

94

The distich shows clearly — shows it despite all *Lust am Protestieren* — where he would have stood, say, in the sixteenth century. In the name of that lofty conception of *Bildung*, in which nature and culture unite, he would have been for Rome against the Reformation — or else he would have taken up an ambiguous and irresponsible position, as Erasmus did, of whom Luther said that repose was dearer to him than the Cross. " The Cross " — a couple of centuries later, that was the Revolution. Revolution was the spirit — and to Goethe his *ruhige Bildung* was dearer.

Here, for a moment, Erasmus and Goethe meet, in an atmosphere of patrician quietism, humanistic love of peace. But the parallel does not long hold — there is too much difference in the scale, and, after all, men's character, the essence of their being, is greatly affected by their proportions. Tolstoy's " folkishness," for instance — is it not the expression and apanage of his bearlike bulk? Are they not one and the same thing? And may we not draw from Goethe's greatness the *a priori* conclusion that his humanistic cosmopolitanism must contain a good-sized racial core? Erasmus, the subtle, was not " folkish." It was Luther who was that. And truly, in scale, in essence, as an embodiment of Germanic greatness, Goethe belongs more with Luther than with the humanists — yes, more even with Bismarck, to whom he is much closer than a certain antithesis, beloved abroad, would seem to show.

Dangerous, perhaps, to say so — as giving aid and comfort to the cave-bears of nationalism the world over — but sometimes it is hard not to feel sceptical about the genuineness and validity of Goethe's humanism. A godlike man, like Tolstoy. But is it possible that the antique, humanistic, Jovelike attributes of his godhead were more a convention than we think; that they did not go very deep, and that he himself, all the time, like Tolstoy, the Russian god under the golden lime-tree, was an ethnic divinity, an eruption of that Germanic and aristocratic paganism which claims both Luther and Bismarck as its sons, and which, on both sides, played a rôle in the ideology of the late war?

An open hostility, against Goethe as well as against Bismarck, is at work in certain literary, humane, and radical circles, a demand for his dethronement. It cannot be without all sense or justification. Goethe, as a follower of Spinoza, conceived of all natural final causes and purposes as anthropomorphic fictions; thus he was disinclined to an anthropocentric, emancipatory conception of humanity, which teleologically refers everything to itself and looks upon art as a servant of mankind. His synthesis of art and nature is not humanitarian. An approach by the route of the senses is natural to him: it makes him see the burning of a peasant house as real and appealing to his sympathies, whereas " the Fall of the Fatherland " he would find an empty phrase. All which, frankly and flippantly spoken, is never very far removed from the brute.

There is in him a feeling for power, for the struggle " until one proves stronger than the other "; in such sentiments the pacifism of spirit would find it impossible to rejoice. It " makes him sad to be friends with everybody." He " needs anger." Certainly, that is not Christian love of

96

peace — though Lutheran it may be, and Bismarckian to boot. One might say much — and much has been said — in evidence of his love of strife, his fondness for " pitching in and punishing," his readiness to close the mouth of opposed opinions by a show of power and to " remove such people from society." But best of all I love — if here too only because it is so amusing — the tale of Kotzebue and the Schiller celebration which Kotzebue got up with the sole and single purpose of annoying Goethe and playing Schiller off against him. That low-minded Kotzebue! He *knows* that the plan will annoy the old man; he also knows that Goethe can forbid the celebration by virtue of his office. So he puts the choice squarely before him: he can forbid it, and thereby betray his jealousy and despotism; or, if he hesitates to go so far, he can pocket up the annoyance. With majestic simplicity Goethe chooses to exercise his power. He *forbids the celebration.* Bismarck would have done the same.

In the soul-economy of this breed of giants are certain parallel traits. There is violence and there is sentimentality: crude words both to describe what I mean, crude and naturalistically derogatory; yet it is my humour to use them; for even if I wanted to I could not ignore the hidden irony — quite objective, quite unsuspected irony, of course — involved in their gigantic loyalties, their aristocratic servitude. They were both " faithful German servants of their Lord " (oh, my God!): the " civilian Wallenstein " and the despot of *Kultur;* they were German *"Edelknechte "* both; and there was nothing hypocritical about it

97

all, only their giant-sensibilities functioning at full height. The similarity of the character and situation is so strong as to bewilder one: Karl August and the simple old man whom Bismarck " served " blend into one single symbolic figure. In the year 1825 he of Saxe-Weimar celebrated the fiftieth jubilee of his reign, which was at the same time the fiftieth year of Goethe's residence in Weimar. On this day Goethe calls himself " his master's most enraptured servant." He is the first with his congratulations, at six o'clock at the Roman villa in the park. The emotion is great and genuine. " Together to our latest breath! " We see the venerable Wilhelm going to meet Bismarck on the landing with just such another embrace; while a fugitive red mounts in the cheeks of Roderich von Posa, who turns away with the words: " I cannot be a courtier! "

I confessed in the beginning my tendency to make a matter of intrinsic value out of the matter of size. The greatest German poet must also be the most German one — that is an association more immediate and inevitable than even the causal, it is temporal, it is simply the future tense. And it was sanctioned by a source which will be universally accepted as authoritative. It was Father Jahn, who, *motu proprio*, in the year 1810 declared that Goethe was the most German of poets — quite unperturbed by the fact that Goethe behaved at all times as distantly and unsympathetically toward *deutsche Bruderschaften* as Tolstoy toward Slavic. And then, in 1813, when he had very nearly succeeded in bringing himself into bad odour as a man without a country, Barnhagen von Ense cried out:

"Goethe not a patriotic German? All the freedom of Germania early found a home in his breast, there to become, to our never-sufficiently-to-be-acknowledged advantage, the pattern, the example, and the root of our culture. In the shade of this tree we all live and move. Never did roots thrust firmer and deeper into the soul of our Fatherland, never did shoots more lustily suck strength from its breast. That our youth feel pride in their arms, loftiness in their spirits, hath more reference to him than to many another who may lay claim to great activity therein."

Good, fine, powerful words. They proceed from the truth that in national matters very little depends on what a man says or the opinions he holds; on what he does, on the other hand, everything. When a man has written *Götz*, *Faust*, *Wilhelm Meister*, the *Sprüche in Reimen* and *Hermann und Dorothea* — a poem which Schlegel honoured with the epithet "*vaterländisch*" — he can indulge in a bit of cosmopolitan irresponsibility, just as the "great writer of Russia" could indulge in the rationalizing Christian pacifism of his latter period. The national is so much second nature that one may address oneself to the mind without running the risk of literary unrealism; and as nature Goethe always felt the national — we see it, among others, in the famous remark to Eckermann: "National hatred is a queer thing after all. You will always find it keenest and most violent *in the lowest stages of culture*. But there is a stage where it quite disappears, and one stands in a way above the nations and feels the well- or ill-being of a neighbouring people as though it were one's own. This stage was conformable to my nature, and I had confirmed myself in it long before I reached my sixtieth year."

Spiritual regeneration. This summons to achieve the spirit is the sentimental imperative of the favourites of nature; just as that of the sons of spirit is the summons to achieve the form. And they respond to it — with more or less of aptitude. Tolstoy's self-imposed task of shaking off the natural man was but spiritualizing the savage; yet a touching and honourable sight, even alongside of Goethe's majestic culture. The main thing is that nothing should come too easy. Effortless nature — that is crude. Effortless spirit is without root — or substance. A lofty encounter of nature and spirit as they mutually yearn toward each other — that is man.

Gorky says of Tolstoy a quite extraordinary and startling thing: he suggests the possibility that Tolstoy, despite the strength of his reason, sometimes hoped, or at least the thought occurred to him, that possibly nature would make an exception, and grant him physical immortality. " The whole broad earth looks toward him: from China, from India, from America, from everywhere stretch hither living, vibrating threads, his soul is for all and for always. Why should not nature break her law, and grant one man physical immortality — why not? " What madness! But even if it is not true, even if the sensible old man never came on such a monstrously presumptuous thought — even so, it is very telling that Gorky should have come on it for him. It shows what seemed to a competent observer to be Tolstoy's relation to nature and life. — And Goethe? Is it likely that the grey-haired lover of Fräulein von Levetzof never rebelled against the limitations of human life, as Napoleon did at the limitations of human power, when he complained that men had become unbelievers, unwilling to acknowledge him a god, as they had his brother Alexander? Shall we imagine him utterly incapable of the thought which Gorky ascribes to the old Tolstoy: that nature might conceivably hesitate to destroy him, her darling son, as she did all ordinary humankind?

Yet die he did, without warning, at the age of eighty-three. Nature, as it were, tenderly got round him. He had been ailing; he settled down in his arm-chair for a rest and a nap, and he was gone. The passage in which Eckermann describes the appearance of the corpse is famous. " The body lay naked, folded in a white sheet; they had put large pieces of ice round, to keep it fresh as long as possible. Friedrich (the servant) unwrapped the sheet, and I was astounded at the godlike splendour of those limbs. The chest exceedingly powerful, broad and deep; the arms and thighs full and gently muscular; the feet slender and very chaste in form; and nowhere on the body a trace of fat or shrinking or decay. A perfect human being lay in great beauty there before me; and the delight I felt made me forget for a moment that the immortal spirit had forsaken such a frame."

Let there be no misunderstanding. Nobody asserts that Goethe and Tolstoy were, so to speak, four-square; that

101

by contrast with the morbid geniuses Schiller and Dostoyevsky they were "normal" in the common acceptation
of the word. Even the genius most endowed by nature is
never natural in the philistine sense; that is to say, normal,
healthy, and according to rule. In his physical there must
always be something high-strung and irritable, prone to
crises and disease, in his psychical always something foreign to the average man, affecting him uncannily — something almost psychopathic; though the philistine must not
be allowed to put it like that. . . . No; what I refer to
here is that *sense-endowment* possessed by the noble race
of Antæus and celebrated by Goethe's Faust in the words
he addresses to the Earth-Spirit:

> *Erhabner Geist, du gabst mir, gabst mir alles,*
> *Warum ich bat. Du hast mir nicht umsonst*
> *Dein Angesicht im Feuer zugewendet.*
> *Gabst mir die herrliche Natur zum Königreich,*
> *Kraft, sie zu fühlen, zu geniessen. Nicht*
> *Kalt staunenden Besuch erlaubst du nur,*
> *Vergönnest mir, in ihre tiefe Brust*
> *Wie in den Busen eines Freunds, zu schauen. . . .*

"Power to feel and to enjoy nature." Tolstoy's sense-
endowment, as an individual, must have been that of a
noble, highly sensitive animal, most perfectly equipped by
nature and strengthened and sublimated by the contempla-
tive power and awareness of the human being. His eyes, the
small, keen grey eyes under the bushy brows, were like a
falcon's. They saw everything. They were capable of analysis so penetrating as sometimes to seem fantastic. A critic

once wrote of him: " You are sometimes capable of saying ' such and such things about the constitution of a certain man indicated that he wanted to travel to India.' " His sense of smell, it seems, was especially penetrating. The fact plays no small part in the sensuous atmosphere of his writing, and appears to have conflicted at times with his own human feeling. " However much I dislike to speak of it," he says in his *Recollections,* " I can still remember the characteristic sharp odour which was personal to my aunt, probably in consequence of some carelessness in dress."

I have already spoken of Goethe's sensitiveness to weather conditions. It was due to his almost exaggerated sense-endowment; and became positively occult when that night in his chamber in Weimar he felt the earthquake of Messina. Animals have a nervous equipment which enables them to feel such events when they occur and even beforehand. The animal in us transcends; and all transcendence is animal. The highly irritable sense-equipment of a man who is nature's familiar goes beyond the bounds of the actual senses and issues in the suprasensual, in natural mysticism. With Goethe the divine animal is frankly and proudly justified of itself in all spheres of activity, even the sexual. His mood was sometimes priapic — a thing which of course does not happen with Tolstoy, in whose nature the element of antique culture was missing. In him the voice of sexual desire spoke in no classic accents; it revelled Russianly in its strength; yet at the same time it always had a moral cast, was at all times followed, probably even accompanied, by profound remorse. Tolstoy's comrades from his Sebastopol period bear witness to the fury with which even at that time the battle between sensual and spiritual impulses raged within him. According to them young Count Tolstoy was a glorious comrade, the life and soul of his battery, overflowing with high spirits. When he was away, they were disconsolate. " We would hear nothing of him," says the narrator, " for a whole day, for two or three days. At last he would come back, the very picture of the prodigal son; gloomy, knocked up, out of sorts with himself. He would take me aside and begin to confess. He confessed everything, simply everything, his gambling, his carousing, where he had spent his days and nights — and, would you believe it, his remorse and suffering were as deep as though he had committed some great crime. His despair went so beyond all bounds that it was painful to behold. That was the sort of man he was. He was, in a word, very remarkable, and, to tell the truth, I never did quite understand him."

That we can well believe. The remorse and suffering to which the young officer was a witness sprang of course from that conflict within Tolstoy's own breast which after-wards gave him such unrivalled power to stir the conscience and prick man's fear of God awake. But the depth of his moral necessity is a precise measure of the violence of his instincts; and though his natural man bore heavier and heavier on his Christianity as time went on, so that he craved surcease from its stings, yet he never, up till the end, attained to peace. Tolstoy in sex matters held out as long as Goethe, who mocked himself thus:

Alter, hörst du noch nicht auf?
Immer, Mädchen!

But his state of mind toward woman, whom he had early learned to regard, after the manner of the Fathers, as *instrumentum diaboli,* had long since assumed such a form that an experience like that of Goethe with Ulrike was unthinkable. Stranger still — or no, in a man of his parts and magnificence it is only what we should expect — we find not a trace of cant or prudishness or even delicacy in all his recorded utterances on this subject. On the contrary, they are all of a pagan frankness that borders on the cynical. He goes walking by the sea with Gorky and Anton Tschekof, and suddenly he levels at Tschekof a question about the latter's youth, using a crude Biblical word with rather startling effect. Anton Pavlovich is confused; he pulls at his little beard and mutters something in reply. The old man lets him stammer awhile, then, looking out to sea, delivers himself in four words, of a confession of his own, in good round terms, ending with a very low and vulgar peasant word. " When they come from his rugged lips," says Gorky, " words like that lose their barrack-room flavour and sound quite simple and natural."

Again, he says: " If Leo Nikolaevich were a natural scientist, he would certainly evolve the most ingenious hypotheses, and make the greatest discoveries." Gorky has not here in mind Tolstoy's remarkable sense-equipment; but I am inclined to associate the two ideas. Nor, it would appear, has he Goethe in mind when he ascribes to Tolstoy a latent genius for the natural sciences; but I have. To me

105

it seems a pertinent fact that Goethe, in Venice — this was in 1790, at the time of those amorous adventures celebrated in the *Epigrams* — saw a broken sheep-skull on the Lido, and had that morphological insight into the development of all the bones of the skull out of the vertebræ which shed such important illumination upon the metamorphosis of the animal body. When Gorky says that Tolstoy, if he had gone in for it, would have made brilliant discoveries in the field of natural science, there can be no doubt of his meaning. He has in mind that initiated sympathy with organic life which those must possess who are her favoured sons — a sympathy not far from Eros, and in which Goethe's biologic intuitions have their source; for example, his incredibly sure-footed anticipation of the cell theory.

Does it not find expression, this sympathy, in the youthful Goethe's Ganymede-pathos? " *Mit tausendfacher Liebeswonne sich an mein Herz drängt deiner ewigen Wärme heilig Gefühl.*" . . . " *Aufwärts an deinen Busen, allliebender Vater!* " Does it not find expression in his pantheism, which is only the objectivation of his feeling, in such wise that his own utter surrender gives him to know the divine not as something from without, but as irradiating him through and through? In any case, this organic sympathy, this living interest, is entirely directed toward life, toward the " *ewige Wärme* "; whereas — and what could be more characteristic of the difference between these two, nature's great children? — Tolstoy's strongest, most tormenting, deepest, and most productive interest has to do with death. It is the thought of death which dominates his thoughts and writing, to such an extent that one may say no other great master of literature has felt and depicted death as he has — felt it with such frightful penetration, depicted it so insatiably often. Tolstoy's poetic genius for questioning death is the pendant to Goethe's intuition in the field of natural science; and sympathy with the organic is at the bottom of both. Death is a very sensual, very physical business; and it would be hard to say whether Tolstoy was so interested in death because he was so much and so sensually interested in the body, and in nature as the life of the body, or whether it was the other way about. In any case, in his fixation with death, *love* comes into play too: for the fear of death, this source of Tolstoy's poetry and his feeling for religion, is fear of the love of nature, it is the negative, naturalistic other side of Goethe's Ganymede-impulse.

" *Du führst,*" says Goethe-Faust to the Earth-Spirit:
" *Du führst die Reihe der Lebendigen*
   Vor mir vorbei und lehrst mich meine Brüder   .
   Im stillen Busch, in Luft und Wasser kennen."
" My brothers." We know that it was Goethe who took in all seriousness the idea of " man's close relation to the beast," and that before science had got far enough on to do so; his possession by this thought, this profound and true intuition, shows us the child of nature in all his sympathy with the organic. Schiller's humanity, his conception of man, which was at bottom emancipatory, haughtily inimical to nature, would have found little pleasure in such

107

a conception; and one does not discover ideas to which one is unsympathetic; that is to say, ideally unsympathetic. There is not such a thing as an assumptionless science. Scientific discoveries are always the result of an ideal assumption: the mediæval statement " *Credo ut intellegam* " is eternally right. Belief is the organ of knowledge; and without the preconceived, previsioned idea of a unified plan on which is based the development of the higher vertebrate world, including man — in the plant world the conception of the " primitive plant " — Goethe never would have found the *os intermaxillare* in man. I may speak of the amusing contradiction between his discovery and the humanistic explanation he gave it. He says that the intermaxillary bone is variously shaped, in animals, according to circumstance and necessity; but that when it came to man, the highest in the scale, it hid itself for shame, " afraid of betraying an animal voracity." Ideal human pride might retort that it was truly inhuman to spy out the shamefaced hidden bone and bring it to the light.

Yet how remarkable and significant it is to see Goethe's medical and biological interest being seasoned from the start with the humanistic, with his concern with man and his beauty! And consequently with art too; since art with Goethe was a humanistic discipline, and all the disciplines and faculties of human endeavour, human wisdom, human power, were seen by him as variations and adumbrations of one and the same great compelling and enchanting interest and concern, which is man. To study humanity from the angle of medicine and the natural sciences did not lie in

his family tradition, as it did in Schiller's and Dostoyevsky's, both of whom were sons of physicians, and neither of
whom gave a thought to man's physical side. On the other
hand, we know that ever since his Leipsic days Goethe had
occupied himself with medicine, associated every day with
medical men in Strasburg, worked in the dissecting-rooms,
spent time in the obstetrical clinic and the clinic for
internal diseases. The spirit in which he pursued these
studies, the kind of interest he took in them, is clear from
the fact that he himself later in life lectured to young artists in the academy on the bony structure of the body. The
same thing comes out even plainer in the words he puts into
the mouth of Wilhelm Meister in the *Wanderjahre,* when
the hero takes his surgical training. His primary interest
is in anatomy; and we get some very curious information
on the point of previous preparation in a quite different
field of activity.

"By a peculiar method, which no one would guess, I
had already made good progress in knowledge of the
human frame; and this was during my theatrical career.
When you come down to it, the physical man, after all,
plays the principal rôle there — a fine man, a fine woman!
If the manager is lucky enough to have got hold of these,
the writers of comedy and tragedy are assured. The free
footing upon which such society lives makes their associates
more familiar with the peculiar beauty of the uncovered
limbs than any other relationship; different costumes often
oblige them to make visible what otherwise is generally
concealed. On this point I might have much to say, as also

109

of physical defects which the sensible actor must recognize in himself or others, in order, if not to correct, at least to hide them. In this way I was sufficiently prepared to give consistency to the anatomical course which taught me to know the outer parts more accurately, whilst the inner parts too were not strange to me, inasmuch as a certain perception of them had always been present to me."

This is, I repeat, a significant bit of information. We learn, not only that the acquaintance with the human form, which Wilhelm owed to the " free footing " of theatrical life, was a happy preparation for his anatomical studies; but also that both, his leaning to the theatre and his interest in medicine, were expressions of one and the same profound interest, his sympathy with the organic and its highest revelation, the human form — an interest, and a sympathy, not far removed, as I said, from Eros. For instance, when Wilhelm Meister, one day in the dissecting-room, finds that his subject is " the most beautiful female arm that ever twined itself about a young man's neck " — and cannot bring himself to mutilate with his instruments this " glorious manifestation of nature." Out of this incident there comes about his acquaintance with that remarkable man, the " plastic anatomist," a sculptor who prepares from wax or other material anatomical dissections possessing the fresh colour and appearance of the natural subjects, in the hope of employing his ingenuity and fertility of method to make the demonstrations more valuable to students and medical practitioners the world over. There follow the most pregnant conversa-

110

tions upon the association of plastic art and anatomical knowledge, and the two intertwine in the most wonderful way when the master " cast in a shaped mass the beautiful torso of a youth and now was skilfully trying to divest the ideal form of the epidermis, to change the beautiful shapes of life into a veritable preparation of muscular tissue."

Here the prose work of Goethe's later period refers to his own youthful thoughts and experiences as a student. He had early discovered and stated that a knowledge of nature and a knowledge of art reciprocally heighten each other. " As I observe nature," he wrote from Rome, " so I now observe art, and win what I have so long striven after, a perfect conception of the highest that has been accomplished by man; and *my soul gets formed* more on this side and looks into a freer field." " Architecture and sculpture and painting are to me now like mineralogy, botany, and zoology," he says in a letter to Herder. And again: " We can finally rival nature by the use of art only when we have learned from her, at least to some extent, the way she proceeds in the formation of her works. . . . The human form cannot be comprehended merely by looking at the surface of it; one must lay bare its inwardness, disjoin its parts, observe the connexion between them, note the dissimilarities, be instructed in the action and counteraction, print upon one's mind the hidden and dormant and basic features of a phenomenon, if one wants really to see and imitate it as it moves, a beautiful, indivisible whole, in living waves before our eyes." These are Goethe's words, and who could doubt their truth? Who would deny that it advantages the artist to have knowledge of something beneath the skin, so that he can paint what is not seen as well as what is: in other words, if he stand to nature in another relation besides the lyrical, if, for example, he is a physician on the side, a physiologist, an anatomist, and quietly knows what he knows about the *dessous* as well? The envelope of a human body consists not only of the mucous membrane and cornea of the epidermis, but underneath one has to imagine the corium with its oil and sweat glands, bloodvessels and tubercles, and under that again the adipose tissue, the upholstery that lends the form its charm. But what the artist knows and thinks tells too: it flows into his hand and has its effect; it is not there and yet somehow it is, and just this it is that gives perspicuousness. Art, I repeat, is only one humanistic discipline among others; all of them, philosophy, jurisprudence, medicine, theology, even the natural sciences and technology as well, are only variations and subspecies of one and the same high and interesting theme — toward which we can never take up a sufficiently varied and many-sided attitude, for it is man; and the *human form* is the summary of them all, it is, to speak with Goethe, " the *non plus ultra* of all human knowledge and activity, the alpha and omega of all things known unto us."

Autobiography, and education. The two conceptions meet again when we envisage this idea of the human form, this loftiest expression of our sympathy with the organic. Yes, in view of this idea, so genuinely creative, the two con-

112

ceptions flow into one humane whole: the pedagogic element resides, consciously or unconsciously (and if unconsciously, so much the better), in the autobiographic;
it follows from it, it grows out of it.

Goethe somewhere calls Wilhelm Meister his "beloved
likeness (*sein geliebtes Ebenbild*)." In what sense? Does
a man love his own likeness? Unless he suffer from hopeless self-complacency, should not the sight of it make him
aware of his own shortcomings? Yes, of course, it should.
And this very awareness of a need of improvement and
completion, this consciousness of his own ego as a task,
a moral, æsthetic, cultural obligation, becomes objective
in the hero of the autobiographical novel, the epic of education. To this personage the creative ego acts as guide,
philosopher, and friend — at once identical and superior —
to an extent that makes Goethe once refer to his Wilhelm
as "a poor dog." The phrase bespeaks a parental tenderness, not only toward the poor fellow in his *dunklen Drange*
whom he created in his own image, but also toward himself. And thus, at the very heart of the autobiographic
pathos there takes place the turn for the pedagogic. And
this process of objectivation goes on in Wilhelm Meister
through the introduction of the society of the Turm, which
takes in hand his destiny and human development and
leads him in mysterious ways. More and more plainly
in the *Lehrjahre* does the original idea of a personally conducted adventure in self-improvement tend toward the pedagogic; until in the *Travels* it issues entirely in the social,
yes, even in the political. At the end of the *Faust* there is

113

an unmistakable flashing-up in poetry of the same vision of the union of self and society in the educational process. For the Enlightened, who on earth " *immer strebend sich bemüht,*" is received on high by the youthful saved, who sing:

> " *Wir wurden früh entfernt*
> *Von Lebechören;*
> *Doch dieser hat gelernt,*
> *Er wird uns lehren.*"

Nobody has ever loved his own ego, nobody was ever egocentric, in the sense of conceiving of his own ego as a cultural task and toiling early and late in pursuance of it, without reaping, almost as though by accident, educational influence in the outer world, and the joy and dignity of a leader and former of youth. The harvest never comes save at the height of life, and the moment of his realization of it is the sublime moment in the life of the productive human being. He never foresees, or even suspects, the moment beforehand. The autobiographical " poor dog," with his mind from his youth up wholly on the difficulties of ploughing his own furrow, or, in the religious phrase, on the saving and justification of his own soul, will not have imagined he can teach anything, to improve or to convert men. Yet the day comes when, still incredulous, still astonished, he realizes that he has been teaching while he learned — shaping, guiding, leading, training, putting his own stamp on youth, by the power of words, by that lofty instrument of culture which is Eros-filled and binds the hearts of men. And from the day of his realization this knowledge pos-

114

sesses his whole life with a certainty, a creative bliss which
leaves far behind it all ordinary human joys of love and
fatherhood — just as the life of the mind is wont to ex-
ceed all personal and sensual things in value, beauty, and
splendour.

"I am reading Goethe. My mind teems," Tolstoy wrote
in his journal at the beginning of the sixties. He was then
a man of some thirty years and had not long returned to
Russia and begun his work as a preaching and practising
pedagogue. What was he reading? Was it contact with German idealism and humanism that made his mind so to
"teem"? It was an alien sphere to him. For in Tolstoy
(otherwise than in Goethe), the origin of the pedagogic
impulse was immediately social and ethical. A man of parts
and attainments, said he, must share with those who lack
such blessings before he can derive pleasure from them
himself. The motive seems a poor one to me; rationalizing
and humanitarian, like all the conscious thought of the
great artist just then, I find it deeply inferior to the beautiful humanity of Goethe, in whom the social ideal was an
organic outgrowth of the cultural and educational. But
what Tolstoy thought was usually smaller than what he was.
And to come back to our starting-point: what was it made
his mind "teem" when he read Goethe and at the same
time set to work as single-handed schoolmaster and founder
of a primary school to put into practice the pedagogic ideas
that rumbled in his belly?

Or, rather, to experiment with them. For he had made up

115

his mind to settle, by actual experiment, what it was that the people, and in particular youth, wanted to be taught; it had not been settled, and that it had to be settled was his primary pedagogical thesis. " The people," he said, " this most interested party in the whole situation, party and judge in one, listens quietly to our more or less ingenious exposition as to the best way of preparing and presenting its mental fodder. It is not disturbed; for it perfectly knows that in the great business of its mental development it will never take a false step, or accept anything that is false; and that all efforts to force it into paths unsuited to it, for instance German paths, will be like water on a duck's back." One must recognize, Tolstoy declares in writing and controversy, that the German type of school is a desirable one; that is a fact for which history vouches. But, even so, one may as a Russian hesitate to enter the lists in favour of a primary school which does not yet exist there. What historical argument can be brought for the assertion that Russian schools must be like those in the rest of Europe? The people, he says, need education, and every human being seeks it unconsciously. The more highly cultivated classes, society, and government officials, seek to extend the benefits of their knowledge and to educate the less educated masses. One would suppose that such a concurrence of the needs of both classes, the giving as well as the receiving, would suffice. But no. The masses steadily oppose all efforts made in their behalf to educate them, so that these are often entirely futile. Whose is the fault? Which is more justified: the opposition, or the sys-

116

tem against which it is directed? Must the opposition be broken or the system altered? The latter, Tolstoy decides, is the case. " Shall we not," he asks, " confess honourably and openly that we do not, cannot, know what the needs of the coming generations will be; but that we feel none the less bound to investigate? That we will not charge the masses with ignorance because they will not accept our education; but rather accuse ourselves of both ignorance and arrogance if we go on trying to educate them on our own lines? Let us at last cease to see hostility in the resistance of the people to our system; and find in it the expression of the people's will, which alone should guide us. Let us at last accept the fact, so clearly evinced by the whole history of pedagogics, that if the educating class are to know what is good and what bad, the class to be educated must have full power to register dissatisfaction, and opportunity to reject a system which they instinctively find unsatisfying; that, in short, *freedom* is the sole criterion of educational methods."

" The sole criterion of education is freedom, the sole method experience, experimentation." This is Tolstoy's first and highest pedagogic maxim. According to him, the school should be at once a means of education and an experiment performed on the rising generation, an experiment productive of ever new results. It should, in other words, be an educational laboratory, where the experiment of pedagogic science seeks to create a firm basis for itself. To do this, it is necessary that it function under circumstances that ensure the value of its results — that is, in freedom. The school as it is, Tolstoy declares, enfeebles the children by distorting their mental faculties. During the most precious period of development it wrenches the child out of the family circle, robs him of the joy of freedom, and makes of him a jaded, suppressed creature, upon whose face rests an expression of weariness, fear, and boredom, while with his lips he repeats strange words in a language he does not know. But if we give the people freedom during their training, then we also give them the chance to speak out on the score of their necessities, and furthermore to choose among the kinds of knowledge offered. Philosophers from Plato to Kant have unanimously striven to free the school from the fetters of tradition. They have sought to discover wherein the intellectual needs of man consist, and to build up new schools on these more or less correctly envisaged needs. Luther demands that the masses shall study the Scripture from the original text, and not from the commentaries of the Fathers. Bacon advises the study of nature from nature herself and not from the works of Aristotle. Rousseau wants to teach life *from life*, as he conceives it, and not from outworn experience. All philosophy stands for freeing the school from the idea of instructing the younger generation in that which the older generation held to be science; and in favour of the idea of teaching them what they themselves need. And we can see by the history of pedagogic science that every step forwards consists in greater natural *rapport* between pupil and teacher, in less compulsion and greater facilitation of the process of learning.

118

Tolstoy, then, an anarchistic pedagogue, sets his face against discipline. " The school in which there is less compulsion," he says, " is better than the one in which there is more. The method which can be introduced without increased disciplinary strain is good; one which requires greater severity is surely wrong. Take a school like mine and try to carry on conversations about tables and corners of rooms or shove little dice to and fro. A frightful disorder will reign at once, and it will be absolutely necessary to restore order. But tell them an interesting story or set them an interesting task, or let someone write on the board and the others correct, and *let them all out of their benches,* and they will all be busy, and there will be no mischief, and no increased discipline will be necessary. We may safely say that this way is good."

" The children bring nothing with them," thus Tolstoy describes the procedure at Yasnaya Polyana, " neither primers nor copy-books. There are no tasks to take home. They need not remember anything — nothing of what they did the day before. They need carry nothing, either in their hands or in their heads. They bring nothing with them but their receptive natures and the conviction that school will be just as jolly today as it was yesterday; they only think of the instruction when it has begun. No one who comes late is ever scolded, and they never come late, except some of the older ones, whose fathers occasionally keep them to work. When that happens, they run as fast as they can to school and get there breathless."

Lucky village children of Yasnaya Polyana! But it is

119

comprehensible that Tolstoy tries to make the school at least pleasant for his pupils; his faith in its educational value is weak, and he makes in the end no secret of his conviction — which he declares he derived from personal observation in the schools of Paris, Marseilles, and other cities of western Europe — that the greater part of popular education is gained, not from school, but from life; and that free public instruction, by means of lectures, clubs, books, exhibitions, and so on, remains far superior to any teaching in schools. But be that as it may; what interests us here is not the rightness or wrongness of Tolstoy's ideas, but rather what is characteristic in them; and characteristic they certainly are, in the highest degree, and from every point of view, not only in a personal sense, but also as a sign, even as an augury of his time.

What strikes one first of all, then, is a note that sounds in clearest contradiction to certain other of his doctrines: to the pacifistic and antinational ones, to the thesis of democratic equality he preached in his latter days. It is the national note. He emphasizes the right of the Russian people to an education suited to their genius, independently of the foreign spirit. His root-and-branch Russianism, at this time still quite unregenerate, denies the right of the upper and official classes, with their west-European liberal education, to force upon the masses an education not suited to their actual needs. Here he is turning against Peter the Great, who created these official classes and gave them their orientation toward liberalism and the west. Tolstoy's educational ideas are all extreme anti-" Petrinic," anti-western, anti-progressive. He openly declares that the educated class is not capable of giving the masses their proper training, conceiving, as it does, that the well-being of the people lies in the direction of civilization and progress. What speaks out of Tolstoy's mouth, what rules his thinking, is Moscow. It is that leaning toward Asia which so alarmed Turgeniev and others like him in Tolstoy's writings and which here is elevated to a pedagogic principle. His anarchism, his faith in the anarchistic principle as the single reasonable basis of communal human life; his doctrine that absolute freedom makes all discipline superfluous — all these are part of it, and it and they are expressed in Tolstoy's prescription to " let all the children out of the benches " and free them from every oppressive sense of duty.

This " *letting all the children out of the benches* " — a picturesque and stimulating formula — is a perfect symbol for Tolstoy's social and political (or, rather, his anarchistic, antipolitical) views. His famous letter to Czar Alexander III develops these most concisely. The new Czar's father had been murdered on the first of March 1881; and Tolstoy wrote begging him to exercise clemency toward the murderers. He here sets down for the Emperor, in words so compelling that one almost wonders at their not prevailing, the two *political* expedients which had been applied up to date against increasing political disorder: first, force and terror; and second, liberalism, constitution, parliament. Both these have finally shown themselves impotent. There remains, however, a third expedient, which is not of a political nature and which has at least the

121

advantage of having never yet been tried. It consists in the fulfilment of the divine will regardless of consequences, without any cautious reservations of policy; quite simply in love, forgiveness, the requital of evil with good; in mildness, in non-resistance against evil, in freedom. . . . In a word, Tolstoy advises the Czar to " let all the children out of the benches "; he counsels anarchy — I am not using the word in a derogatory sense, but quite objectively, to specify a definite social and political gospel of salvation.

The Asiatic bias of this great Russian genius has already been shown to be a mixture of various psychical elements: oriental passivity, religious quietism, and an unmistakable tendency to Sarmatian wildness. Here, in this anarchistic theory, it lies down with quite different company: with the revolutionary ideals of western Europe, with the educational and political conceptions of Rousseau and his pupil Pestalozzi, in both of whom there is present the element of wildness, the return to nature — in short, the anarchistic element in another form and under other colours. Here, then, we are arrived at the common factor in the education of our two protagonists — but with a difference. On the educational side, Goethe fell away from his allegiance to Rousseau. Pedagogic Rousseauianism, as preached and practised by its founder, revolted him. Furiously, even desperately, he rejected it, and the anarchical individualism of the revolutionary education.

Boisserée tells how Goethe expressed to him his distress on the score of Pestalozzi and his system. For its original

122

purpose and in its original setting, where Pestalozzi had only the children of the people in mind, the poor who lived in their isolated huts in Switzerland and could not send their children to school, it might be a capital idea. But it became the most destructive one in the world so soon as it ceased to confine itself to elementary teaching and went on to language, art, the general field of knowledge and power, which of course presupposed a *previous tradition.* . . . And then the insubordination this cursed kind of education aroused: look at the impudence of the little school-urchins, who feel no awe of any stranger, but rather put him in a fright instead. All respect gone, everything done away with that makes human beings human beings in their relations with each other. " What should I have been," cried Goethe, " if I had not always been obliged to show respect for others? And these men, in their madness and frenzy, to reduce everything to terms of the single individual and be simply gods of self-sufficiency! They think to educate a nation which shall stand against the barbaric hordes, just as soon as the latter shall have mastered the elementary tools of understanding, which Pestalozzi has made it so very easy for them to do."

Tradition, reverence — which " makes human beings human beings in their relations with each other " — conformity of the ego within a noble and estimable community; do you not feel the nearness of the Pedagogic Province? Let me recall a moment that dream so wise and splendid, at once austere and blithe, in which can be traced much of the humanism of the eighteenth century, much of

123

the spirit of the *Zauberflöte*, of Sarastro and the " moving toward good with one's hand in a friend's "; and which at the same time contains so much that is new and bold, and, humanly speaking, advanced that it cannot be called less revolutionary than Tolstoy's educational ideas. Only, of course, the anarchistic flavour is utterly lacking; while its conception of humanity and human dignity, culture and civilization, is so consonant with solemn regulation and gradation, with such a pronounced sense of reverence, of traditions, symbols, mysteries, and rhythm, with such a symmetrical, almost choreographic restraint in its freedom, that I may be permitted to call it statesmanlike in the best and finest sense, by way of pointing the contrast to Tolstoy's " letting the children out of the benches." However, the boys and youths of Goethe's dream-province do not sit glued to their benches either, at least we do not see them thus. The basis of their education is quite in the Pestalozzan style: it is husbandry. And their training goes forward in the open air, work and play constantly accompanied by singing. We are told, quite explicitly, what its essence is: " Wise men lead the boys to find out themselves what is fitted for them; and shorten the by-ways into which man will often too readily turn aside." Every well-marked bent to a pursuit is fostered and cultivated, for " to know and practise one thing rightly gives higher culture than half-way performance of a hundred things." But if the education is thus adapted to the individual, it is not thereby in the very least individualistic — so little, in fact, that respect for convention is insisted upon, and regarded as a

124

conspicuous characteristic of genius; for genius understands that art is called art just because it is not nature; and
easily accommodates itself to paying respect to the con-
ventions, in the view that they represent " an agreement
arrived at by the superior elements of society, whereby the
essential and indispensable is regarded as the best." That is
hostility toward the voluntary, with a vengeance; and the
Head is at pains to define and interpret it by a musical
parallel. " Would a musician," he asks, " let a pupil make
a wild attack on the keyboard or invent intervals to please
himself? No, the striking thing is that nothing is left to the
choice of the learner. The element in which he is to work is
fixed, the tool he must use put into his hand, even the way
he shall use it is prescribed — I mean the change of fingers,
in order that one get out of the other's way and make the
path plain for its successor; until by dint of this regulated
co-operation and thus alone the impossible at last becomes
the possible." — It is not by chance, I insist, that the Heads
of the Province draw their parallel from the field of music:
is she not truly the most spirited symbol for that regulated
co-operation of manifold elements toward an end and goal
which is culturally noble and worthy of humanity? In the
Pedagogic Province song presides over all the activities,
everything else is linked with it and communicated by it.
" The simplest pleasures as well as the simplest tasks are
animated and impressed by song; yes, even our instruction
in morals and religion is communicated in this wise."
Even the elements of knowledge, reading, writing, reckoning, are derived from song, note-writing, and putting text

beneath, and from observing the basic measures and nota-
tion — in short, as agriculture is the natural, so music is
the spiritual element of education, " for from it level paths
run out in all directions."

Another great German and shaper of German destiny
comes to mind here: Luther's view of music as an instrument of education was very like Goethe's. " *Musicam*,"
he says, " I have always loved. One should accustom youth
to this art, for it makes fine, capable people. A schoolmaster who cannot sing I will not look at." And in the
schools under his influence there was almost as much singing as in the Pedagogic Province — whereas no one would
know whether they sang in Tolstoy's school or not. To the
wanderer through the Pedagogic Province it seems as
though none of its inhabitants did anything of his own
power, but as though a mysterious spirit animated them
through and through, leading them on toward one single
great goal. This spirit is the spirit of music, of culture,
of " regulated co-operation," whereby alone at length " the
impossible " — that is to say, the state as work of art —
becomes possible; it is a spirit remote from and hostile to
all barbarism; one would like to be allowed to call it a
German spirit.

The salutation in three degrees, whose meaning, the
threefold reverence, is kept secret from the boys themselves, because mystery and respect for the mysterious is a
moral and civilizing influence; the insistence upon modesty
and decorum; the lining up and standing at attention of
the young human being in face of the world, and his

126

honourable comradeship with his kind; the enhancing of
his own honour through the honours he renders; all this
militarism so highly imbued with the spirit and with art
—how far it is from the rational radicalism of Tolstoy's
Christianity, with its heart of wildness! Is it anyway credi-
ble that, in essentials, a remarkable likeness subsists between the educational conceptions of our two geniuses?

Tolstoy in all pious simplicity once declared that the
world can find salvation simply by no longer doing anything which does not seem inherently reasonable: that is
to say, anything which our whole European world is doing
today; for example, teaching the grammar of dead languages. What finds utterance, what bursts forth, in this po-
lemic against the study of ancient tongues is the revolt of the
Russian people against humanistic civilization itself. Tolstoy's unclassic paganism stands revealed, his ethnic godhead, which, according to Gorky, was not Olympian, but
more like that of a Russian god, " sitting on a maple throne,
under a golden lime-tree." Tolstoy's pedagogic writing betrays an extremely anti-humanistic, anti-literary, anti-
rhetorical conception of the relative importance of different branches of study. He has anything but the traditional European view of the importance of the discipline of
reading and writing; entertaining not the faintest humanistic fear of " analphabetism," but rather openly defending what to our way of thinking would almost amount to
a state of barbarism. " We see people," he says, " who are
equipped with all the knowledge necessary for farming;
who perfectly comprehend all its bearings, though they can

127

neither read nor write; or capital military leaders, trades-people, foremen, machine-overseers, labourers, all people who got their training from life, not books, and stored up large resources of information and reflection. On the other hand we see people who can both read and write, but who have not profited by this advantage to learn any new thing." When he dwells upon the conflict between the needs of the people and the learning forced upon them by the ruling classes, he has in mind the fact that the elementary schools are an outgrowth of the higher ones. First the church school, then the higher education, then after that the pri-mary school — a false hierarchy, for it is false that the primary school, instead of conforming to its own needs, should conform — only on a smaller scale — to the de-mands of the higher education. His meaning is clear. He finds the folk-school too literary, too much subordinated to the classical ideal of education, not practical or vital enough, not guided by the principle of training for a calling in life. But we shall be mistaken in expecting from him any greater kindness for either the system or the spirit of the higher institutions of learning. He accuses them of being " entirely divorced from actual life." He compares the true education derived from life itself with that offered to the academic student, and finds that the former produces men capable in their calling, the latter merely " so-called people with a university education — advanced, that is to say irri-table, sickly liberals." He gives " Latin and rhetoric " an-other hundred years of life, not more, and so much only for the reason that " when the medicine has once been bought,

128

one must take it." The phrase betrays plainly enough his attitude toward classical education, toward the traditional European culture, toward humanism. It betrays at the same time his attitude toward the west and civilization, his folkhatred of all that is not of the people, that is foreign, that comes from abroad, that has merely a cultural value — in short, the anger of primitive Russia against Peter the Great.

It is time we looked round in the Pedagogic Province for the place where youth busies itself with the ancient tongues. And, after all, it is rather a shock not to find it. Goethe is not such a barbarian as to despise the study of language or languages, as a cultural instrument. He calls it enthusiastically the most sensitive in the world, and emphasizes its value as a civilizing agent, by having his imaginary pupils take it in connexion with the rude tasks of stable-work; so that, caring for and training animals, they do not become like animals themselves. But the languages here are modern languages. The tongues of various nations are studied in turn — but Latin and Greek, it will be noted, are not in the curriculum.

Well, there are other things which are not expressly mentioned either. But that precisely these subjects should be absent is after all rather striking. Was Goethe a humanist, or was he not? In the first place, his humanism was always of another and a broader kind than merely the philological. And in the second place, the impress of a certain high austerity lies upon all the regulations of the Pedagogic Province, despite the Parnassian blitheness that reigned there. There is no doubt that Goethe, in his consciously

129

pedagogic period, felt, curiously enough, toward the humanistic, Winkelmannian ideal of education much as Tolstoy and Auerbach did about music: a moral severity against the sybaritic, dilettante, the roving and ranging, sipping and changing, which he considered the danger of the " universally human " ideal as applied to pedagogy. He considered this danger more threatening than the peril of specialization and its consequent narrowness and impoverishment — the horrors of which we later comers, to be sure, have learned to know. He espouses the cause of vocational against verbal training, out of the same antiliterary tendency which we observed in Tolstoy; sharing with him the conviction that human culture makes sounder progress by the method of limitation; he is radical enough to use the *Wanderjahre* as a mouth-piece through which to shout " *Narrenpossen* (Stuff and nonsense)! " at the " universally human " educational ideal and " all its works." That is severe. But today, when nobody any longer can live on his income, does it not sound like an uncommonly clear-sighted prophecy when he declares: " Whoever from now on does not take to either an art or a trade will have a hard time of it " ?

I have made no secret of my tendency to interpret the paganism of the children of nature in a primarily ethnical sense. And I am greatly strengthened by this astonishingly radical and decisive rejection, on Goethe's part, of a humane and literary education. Almost I might have dared interpret that gruff " *Narrenpossen!* " as the revolt of Germanic folkishness against the humanistic culture itself.

I have every warrant for asserting that Goethe would have fought like Tolstoy the folly of offering watered scholarship to the people for education — a folly by which one waters the people's sense and spirit, debases and insults, instead of, as one fondly imagines, elevating them! Goethe, who in the *Wahlverwandtschaften* advances — surreptitiously, *" weil die Menge gleich verhöhnet "* — the reactionary and esoteric doctrine: " Bring up the boys to be servants and the girls to be mothers, then all will be well ": was he the man to advocate the breeding of " advanced, that is to say irritable and sickly liberals " ? And was there not perhaps prophetic vision at work in the severity and the limitations of his educational principles? Did his sense of time, like the Russian's, give " Latin and rhetoric " a limit of some hundred years of life? Strange events in our Europe today incline one to regard his maxims in a prophetic light.

The great revolution in Russia brought to the light of day — that light which is so good at illuminating the *surface* of things — the western Marxism which had put its impress upon Tolstoy's country. But it must not blind us to the spectacle of the bolshevist revolution as the end of an epoch: the epoch of Peter the Great, the western, liberalizing, European epoch in the history of Russia, which now, with this revolution, faces eastward once more. It was to no European idea of progress that the Czar fell victim. In him Peter the Great was murdered, and his fall opened to his people not the path toward Europe, but the way home to Asia. But is there not also in western Europe,

precisely since the time of this crisis — whose prophet Leo
Tolstoy was, although Moscow sees it not — is there not
also in western Europe a feeling alive that not only for
Russia, but for it, for us, for all the world there is at
hand the ending of an epoch: the bourgeois, humanistic,
liberal epoch, which was born at the Renaissance and came
to power with the French Revolution, and whose last con-
vulsive twitchings and manifestations of life we are now
beholding? The question is put today whether this Mediter-
ranean, classic, humanistic tradition is commensurate with
humanity and thus coeval with it, or whether it is only the
intellectual expression and apanage of the bourgeois liberal
epoch and destined to perish with its passing.

Europe seems to have answered the question already.
The anti-liberal rebound is more than plain, it is palpable.
It finds political expression in a disgusted turning away
from democracy and parliamentary government, in an
about-face toward dictatorship and terror, executed with
frowning brows. Italian fascism is the precise pendant to
Russian bolshevism; all its archaistic gesturings and mum-
mery cannot disguise its essential hostility to the humane.
And on the Iberian peninsula, where the destruction of the
liberal system was still more obvious than in Italy, things
have taken the same course, even more decisively; military dictatorship has been well established there for some
time. But, indeed, all over Europe — as a consequence of
the war and a sign of an anti-liberal temper — the waters
of nationalism are mightily swollen. The individual peoples
of Europe display a turkey-cock self-assertiveness, a furi-

ous self-deification, in striking contrast to the poverty and prostration of the continent as a whole.

The spiritual destinies of France are remarkable indeed, and of immediate importance to us Germans. In the first years after the war no country seemed more confirmed in the bourgeois-classical tradition. France seemed the one truly conservative country in all Europe. Far from thinking of war as a new revolution, it was bent instead, after the victory and on the basis of the victory, on seeing in it nothing but the confirmation and the consummation of the old, the bourgeois order of 1789. To such questions as the one I have raised above, France made answer with tranquil irony. If Germany, she said, wanted to dream apocalyptic dreams, let her do so by all means; for herself, she felt very comfortable in her classical tradition. Once on the occasion of an international exchange of ideas I had sought to get some of these matters expressed; and I remember how a contributor to the French official newspaper organ answered me that France had always been and would always remain *solidement rationaliste et classique*.

But that was the voice of official, bourgeois, conservative France, not the other France, loftier, young, intellectual, secretly astir. Certainly, this new France is beginning to " dream apocalyptically "; there is of late a good deal of reason to doubt that she feels as much at home as she used to in her tradition. What M. Poincaré, who has no better name for it, knows and hates as " communism " is nothing but the process that is going on there of undermining his bourgeois, classical, old-revolutionary France; the disintegration of the Latin conception of civilization by the action of spiritual ferments which have filtered in from the outside and are doing their work in the blood of the youth — a new, anti-bourgeois, spiritual, and proletarian revolution; and we in Germany think we have ground for hope that, if there are to be atmospheric changes, we too may get a little more air to breathe. For in France the interests of nationalism and of the humanistic culture coincide, in so far as both are based upon the conviction of the absolute supremacy of the Latin civilization and its mission of world-domination as an abiding concern of humanity. Whereas a spirit of European solidarity, and a certain readiness, however conditional, to come to terms with Germany, is more likely to be found on the side of the " communistic " new-revolutionary France, which is no longer quite so sound on the score of its cultural Latinity.

Germany's position, with reference to these phenomena to the west of her, is a difficult and complicated one. For us Germans ourselves, and for the world at large, it is highly important that she see it clearly and recognize it for what it is. For in Germany too there exist the two camps, a humanistic and a " communistic "; from which it follows that two peoples may behave the same, culturally speaking, and reach quite different results, and that there are circumstances under which the pursuance of the same spiritual tendency may be the worst possible method of arriving at political *rapprochement*.

I do not propose to dwell upon German fascism, nor

134

upon the circumstances, the quite comprehensible circumstances, of its origin. It is enough to say that it is a racial religion, with antipathy not only for international Judaism, but also, quite expressly, for Christianity, as a humane influence; nor do its priests behave more friendly toward the humanism of our classical literature. It is a pagan folk-religion, a Wotan cult: it is, to be invidious — and I mean to be invidious — romantic barbarism. It is only consistent in the cultural and educational sphere, where it seeks to check the stream of classical education, to the advantage of the primitive German heritage. And it does not or it will not see what an unhappy pendant it thus funishes to the anti-Latinism of modern-minded France, and how very much it plays into the hands of M. Poincaré, the communist-hater. To profess paganism in Germany today, to worship Odin and hold feasts of the solstice, to conduct oneself like a folk-barbarian, is to prove those French patriots in the right who would like to erect on the Rhine the breastwork of occidental civilization; it is asininely to compromise the position of those Frenchmen who do not make such fine distinctions between Latinity and barbarism, and who are interested in peace, understanding, compromise, and a " gentleman's agreement " with Germany.

This is what I meant when I said that to pursue the same spiritual tendency may be the most wrong-headed of all possible ways for two nations to arrive at a *rapprochement*. Now is not the moment for Germany to make anti-humanistic gestures; to pattern itself upon Tolstoy's pedagogic bolshevism; to characterize as ethnical savagery the rebuke

135

which Goethe administered to the hedonism of the general humanistic ideal in education. No, on the contrary, it is the time for us to lay all possible stress upon our great humane inheritance and to cultivate it with all the means at our command — not only for its own sake, but in order to put visibly in the wrong the claims of Latin civilization. And, in particular, our socialism, which has all too long allowed its spiritual life to languish in the shallows of a crude economic materialism, has no greater need than to find access to that loftier Germany which has always sought with its spirit the land of the Greeks. It is today, politically speaking, our really national party; but it will not truly rise to the height of its national task until — if I may be allowed the extravagance — Karl Marx has read Friedrich Hölderlin: a consummation which, by the way, seems in a fair way to be achieved.

Beautiful is resolution. But the really fruitful, the productive, and hence the artistic principle is that which we call reserve. In the sphere of music we love it as the prolonged note, the teasing melancholy of the not-yet, the inward hesitation of the soul, which bears within itself fulfilment, resolution, and harmony, but denies it for a space, withholds and delays, scruples exquisitely yet a little longer to make the final surrender. In the intellectual sphere we love it as irony: that irony which glances at both sides, which plays slyly and irresponsibly — yet not without benevolence — among opposites, and is in no great haste to take sides and come to decisions; guided as it is by the sur-

136

mise that in great matters, in matters of humanity, every decision may prove premature; that the real goal to reach is
not decision, but harmony, accord. And harmony, in a
matter of eternal contraries, may lie in infinity; yet that
playful reserve called irony carries it within itself, as the
sustained note carries the resolution. In the foregoing
pages I have tried it, this " infinite " irony; and my readers
may judge upon which extreme it more enjoyed playing,
at which side of the eternal contradiction it took keener aim
— and draw their conclusions accordingly; only not too
far-reaching ones!

Irony is the pathos of the middle . . . its moral too, its
ethos. I said that it is not, in general, the German way to be
hasty in deciding the aristocratic problem — if I may, in
this phrase, sum up the whole complex of contrasted values
dealt with in the present essay. We are a people of the
middle, a world-bourgeoisie; there is a fittingness in our
geographical position and in our *mores*. I have been told
that in Hebrew the words for knowing and insight have
the same stem as the word for between.

That German writer who has most urgently pondered upon
the problem of aristocracy was, philologically speaking,
greatly daring when he invented a derivation for the name
of the German people: from *Tiusche-Volk;* that is, *Täusche-
Volk*. But, for all that, the idea is full of esprit. A people
that settles in the bourgeois world-middle must needs be
the *täuschende*, the elusive folk: the race that practises a
sly and ironic reserve toward both sides, that moves between extremes, easily, with non-committal benevolence;

with the morality, no, the simplicity of that elusive " betweenness " of theirs, their faith in knowledge and insight, in cosmopolitan culture.

Fruitful difficulty of the middle, thou art freedom and reserve in one! Let them tell us, as they have told us, that this free-handed policy of ours brings us, in actual practice, to grief. But this practice is doubtful, this disaster even more so. More than probably it came upon us for our own best good; more than probably we were more profoundly striving to bring it about than man ever strives to encompass his happiness. Again, humility in the face of failure is no more noble than humility in the face of success; and nothing but defeatism could shake our faith in the rightness and sanctity of this spiritual attitude of ours, whose end and aim is justified, not as a craving for freedom or as ironic reserve, but as a final synthesis and harmony, the pure idea of man himself.

That mutual character of the sentimental longing — of the sons of spirit for nature, of the sons of nature for spirit (for, as we found, it is not spirit alone that is sentimental) — argues a higher unity as humanity's goal; which she, in very truth the standard-bearer of all aspiration, endows with her own name, with *humanitas*. That instinct of self-preservation, full of reserve as it is, felt by the German people in their central position as a world-bourgeoisie, is genuine nationalism. For that is the name we give to a people's craving for freedom, to the pains they take with themselves, to their effort after self-knowledge and self-fulfilment. So too the artist is loyally and devotedly convinced that his only thought is to wrest his own work and his very own dream out of the block of stone; and yet, in some solemn and moving hour, may learn that the spirit which possessed him had a purer source, that from the stone he carved there is emerging a loftier image than he knew.

Folk, and humanity. It was a seer out of the east, one of those who, like Goethe, Nietzsche, and Whitman, have looked long into the slowly mounting dawn of a new piety — it was Dmitri Merezhkovsky who has said that the animal contains the beast-man and the beast-god. The essence of the beast-god is as yet scarcely comprehended by man, though it is only the union of the beast-god with the beast-man which will some day bring about the redemption of the race of mankind. This " some day," this idea of a redemption, which is no longer Christian and yet not pagan either, carries in itself the solution of the problem of aristocracy, as well as justifying, yes, sanctifying, all ironic reserve on the subject of ultimate values.

We have treated with some assurance of great natures, great creative artists, children of God, in whom the beast-god was strong, as also their sense of self, their feeling for repose, for woman, for the people; we have enjoyed the wit of those world-spirits who tempered and humanized their confessed egotism with a strain of the didactic impulse. More hesitantly we have trenched upon the god-man sphere of those others, their emotional opposites, the men of deeds, the sons of spirit, the saintly and sickly. The true saying of that Russian that the essence of the beast-god is as yet scarcely apprehended by man might strengthen our faith in the ironic doctrine that there is more of grace among those who at bottom " can love nobody but themselves." But well we know that there is no deciding the question which of these two lofty types is called to contribute more and better to the highly cherished idea of a perfected humanity.

1922

II

FREDERICK THE GREAT AND THE GRAND COALITION

FREDERICK THE GREAT AND THE
GRAND COALITION

An Abstract for the Hour

~~~~~~~~~~~~~~~~~~

Well, where shall I begin? The writer of history — and
in this case the historical essayist as well — is always subject to the temptation to which Wagner so magnificently
succumbed when, with no more in view than the presen-
tation of his hero's downfall, he found himself lured by
a pedantic enthusiasm deeper and deeper into his folk-
tale, and urged to include a larger and larger area of his
background, until at last he fetched up against the first
beginnings and origins of all things; and there, at the
lowest E of the prelude to the prelude, he solemnly and
almost soundlessly set to. But both space and time vigor-
ously protest against my following Wagner's example in
this sketch of the origins of a war, the repetition — or con-
tinuation — of which we are seeing today. Rather let me be
strict with myself; and since I must begin somewhere, let
me make my beginning with the profound mistrust, the
deep-seated and, to be quite fair, the rather well-founded
mistrust felt by all the world for Frederick II of Prussia.

Consider: here is a young man, boyish of feature, ele-
gantly built, if rather plump, " the nicest little creature in

the kingdom," a stranger said of him; fresh-coloured, chubby-cheeked, with large, short-sighted, sparkling blue eyes and a nose that made a straight line with his forehead and had a naïve little rosy tip. And this nice young man is a crown prince, with a perfectly well-known past that has been somewhat dissipated and by turns alarming and alarmed; by way of being a *libre-penseur* too, a pert young philosopher and littérateur, author of the highly humanistic *Antimachiavelli*. He is totally unmilitary, so far as can be seen, a civilian of the civilians, even effeminate; runs up bills, and has his heart set on the pomps and vanities. And now this young man becomes king — having proved so devoid of honourable feeling as not to have been provoked by any cudgellings or neck-twistings on the part of his fearsome papa to put a bullet through his brain or even to resign in his brother's favour. And as king so conducts himself that nobody knows what to think. The day that he ascended the throne went for ever after by the name " *La journée des dupes*." Almost everything turned out contrary to expectations. Those who had trembled before the revenge of the new master were not punished, while those who dreamed that their day had come found themselves disillusioned. The poets and fortune-hunters who swarmed round the throne and could not huzza loud or long enough, visibly drew in their horns; and a jolly fellow from Rheinsberg, who knew no better than to strike up confidently in the key of former days, received a sparkling blue glance and the cutting words: " *Monsieur, à présent je suis roi*." In other words, the joke is played out. It

144

is precisely the scene in Shakespeare, perhaps the finest in the whole of him, where somebody, with just such a look, says to somebody else: " I know thee not, old man."

Some things which the youth does in his very first days of power have literary *habitus,* are rather high-handed and self-assertive. He abolishes the torture — so much the better for the thieves! He declares that the gazettes need not be afraid to be a little amusing, they will not be prosecuted; and annuls the censorship (and puts it back a year later). He proclaims religious toleration — that is his much-talked-of enlightenment, of course. But what has become of that dream of Parnassus, that court of the muses, where fashion and wit should reign and all be careless, voluptuous, and gallant? It is nowhere at all. The new lord turns out to be, of all things in the world, a rigid economist. No rise in the pay of officials. No reduction of the high tariffs, however much certain people may have counted on relief. The chancelleries of the kingdom are notified that the financial system of his dear departed Majesty will continue strictly in force. Finance-Minister Boden, a much-hated skinflint, remains in office. There is no such thing as trust, or easy-going, or *laissez-aller.* Everybody is watched as never before. And Baron von Pöllnitz actually said, with a sigh: " I'd give a hundred pistoles to have the old man back again! "

No revolutionary changes of system, then. No loosening of the reins of government, no new faces in the Ministry. But one thing, at least, will surely be different: this is a civilian of civilians who reigns, he stands for literature and silk dressing-gowns and a definite end to Potsdam militarism. Surely the corporal's baton has gone out of fashion! Well, just here everybody gets the greatest surprise of all. The slack and rather sensual young philosopher comes out as an impassioned soldier: he has no thought of weakening the military basis of the State. Weaken it? He strengthens the army by fifteen battalions, five squadrons of hussars (introduced on the Austrian model), and a squadron of *gardes du corps,* bringing it up to a round ninety thousand men. The uniform once cursed and jeered at he is never seen out of. His conservatism extends to the retention of all the existing military ranks. " The army organization is a monument of His Majesty our dearly beloved father's wisdom in government; it is, in essentials, not to be tampered with." A few barbarities in the recruiting system are done away with: the flogging of cadets, maltreating the common man, have to be frowned on for his credit's sake. But that is all. What seems to need change is the *meaning* of the institution, the spirit in which it is employed — its political significance, in short. And just here is the suspicious thing.

The military had been something like a foible of the deceased sovereign, a barbaric and rather costly fad, a laughing-stock at all the courts of Europe, where it had never weighed in the scale of affairs. All at once it becomes " the power of the State " — Frederick's phrase in one of his first letters as ruler — a curiously practical conception, further borne out by the way he sets to work to purge the establishment of the quaint flourishes it had as a fad of the deceased King. The regiment of giants, a sight worth looking at, but not good for much else, is done away with, appears for the last time at the funeral ceremonies of Frederick William. Only a battalion of grenadier guards is left, for the sake of filial piety. " The power of the State." Prussia's representatives at foreign courts begin suddenly to speak a language that makes one doubt one's ears. Prussia takes the stage; Prussia unmistakably means to be treated as the not negligible entity she really is. Her astonishing young king behaves as though Prussia were not so much a state of the German empire as a European one. He lets it be known that he is not minded for ever to span the bow and never to let it go, as Europe has long mocked at Prussia for doing.

But what shall we make of all this? Had he been a comedian all this time? Count Seckendorff once wrote about him to Vienna when he was still crown prince: " His greatest fault is his dissimulation and falseness, which makes it necessary to exercise the very greatest caution in what one tells him." Yes, that is evidently true. Seckendorff goes on: " He told me he was a poet, he could write a hundred lines in an hour. And a musician too, a moral philosopher, a physicist, a mechanic. What he never will be is a statesman or a commander-in-chief." Looked at from this end, it seems as though the young man had deliberately dissimulated in this respect as well. For the last surprise is the greatest of all; for the first time it betrays what is actually to be expected of him.

Frederick has not been on the throne for half a year when Charles VI dies; and scarcely is the Emperor below ground when Frederick, to the great consternation of his own ministers, generals, and relatives and the rest of the world as well, lays some sort of claim to Silesia. By the letter of the law and by virtue of solemn compacts, the claim is wholly unfounded; or, if you like, founded on the divers acts of perfidy and presumption which Brandenburg has had from time immemorial to endure from Austria. In any case it is a claim which Frederick, unless Maria Theresa acquiesces, and that she cannot possibly do, is prepared to maintain with the sword. " Everything is in readiness," he writes to Algarotti; " I have only to put into effect the plans I have had a long time in my head." A long time? And everything in readiness? Without saying a word to a soul? Without betraying by the smallest sign that he had such ideas in his head? Well, he has certainly been a dissembling, reserved, solitary young man, all the conviviality on the Remusberg to the contrary notwithstanding! To Voltaire, on the other hand, he writes: " The Emperor's death upset all my peaceful ideas." This in order that Voltaire in France might not suppose that the attack had been a matter of long preparation. Oh, a young man both particularly solitary and particularly sly!

However, there it is: Frederick invades the imperial domains — he, Margrave of Brandenburg, who, as hereditary arch-chamberlain, has had to hand the wash-basin to Maria Theresa's ancestors. " *C'est un fou, cet homme là est fol*," said Louis XV, who after all must have known something about the game of politics. A piece of bravado, a perfectly reckless beginning, says all Europe. And the

148

English Minister in Vienna is even then of the opinion that Frederick ought to be outlawed.

But bravado or no — Austria is in bad form, things turn out well for Frederick. There is the battle of Mollwitz, where he is beaten and takes to his heels for ten miles, while Schwerin comes up and wins the day for him. Not a glorious day for the King, but a victory none the less. Then Bavaria has hankerings after the imperial crown, France supports her, Austria is hard pressed. On top of that comes Chotusitz, where Buddenbrock throws the Austrians into the burning village; and Maria Theresa, who would rather lose a whole province to Bavaria than a single village to Prussia (she hates this Frederick with the whole strength of her femininity), must, anguish in her white bosom, tears in her blue eyes, sign a peace that assures to the King Upper and Lower Silesia and the Duchy of Gratz. He has them, they are his.

What else? A round two years have passed when Frederick makes war again — ostensibly as an elector of the realm to bring succour to the hard-pressed Bavarian emperor, but actually because Maria Theresa has meanwhile been rather too successful against France and Bavaria, and Frederick suspects that when she has finished with the others she will turn round and take Silesia away from him again: beautiful, never-to-be-forgotten Silesia — she bursts into tears whenever she hears it mentioned. And she is not without powerful friends: for instance, King George II of England, conqueror of the French and ally of the Empress-queen since Worms, 1734. King George wrote to her in these very words: "*Madame, ce qui est bon à prendre est bon à rendre*" — the letter fell into Frederick's hands. England and Austria have helped each other defend the territories which each had possessed up to 1739. Up to 1739? That was, to be sure, before Frederick took Silesia. And there are similar pacts entered into between Austria and Saxony. The Austrian historians call heaven to witness that the Empress had not at that time planned any attack, but it was enough for Frederick. He stood very well with France: since June he had had with Richelieu a twelve-year offensive alliance; he is not without diplomatic safeguards. In these two years he has increased the "power of the State" by eighteen thousand "moustaches," as Voltaire called them; greatly strengthened and rebuilt the Silesian fortresses; and in the middle of the summer of '44 he strikes again, without even declaring war; falls upon Bohemia eighty thousand strong, marches through Saxony without even asking the Elector's leave, marches toward Prague, marches actually against Vienna.

It is heavy going. Now and then things look desperate. Charles of Lorraine hurls himself from Alsace into Bohemia and threatens Frederick's Silesian connexions; the Saxon army has the King in the rear — there is an awkward retreat, due to several foolish decisions on Frederick's part, by his own later confession — he learned much from them. By the next year his generalship shows itself devilishly improved! Soor follows on Hohenfriedberg; after he has annihilated the Saxons at Kesselsdorf, Count Harrach comes as broker to Dresden, and Maria Theresa confirms the cession of Silesia, while Frederick recognizes her husband, the gallant Francis of Lorraine, as German emperor. Why not? — Charles VII is dead, and Frederick never set great store by him anyhow.

But why does he make peace with Habsburg? Because he sees that fortune has been with France in the Netherlands, and so, for the present, the Empress-queen's preponderance is not very great. Also, to the huge dissatisfaction of France, he makes peace with England too, withdraws with his booty — Silesia — and sagely resists for the next three years — for so long does the War of the Pragmatic Sanction go on between France and Austria supported by the sea powers — all attempts to draw him out of his neutrality. By the Peace of Aix-la-Chapelle, which finally brought the struggle to an end in favour of Maria Theresa, he gets his Silesian " acquisition " expressly guaranteed.

But one thing we must say: if the Silesian " acquisition " be considered robbery, a piece of property snatched in defiance of justice — and people did so consider it, and so it was — then they should not have solemnly guaranteed it to the robber. That they did so guarantee it meant that they left it to time to right the wrong (as time can do) and that Europe and Maria Theresa from then on renounced all machinations and conspiracies against the robber, and accepted the *fait accompli*. But this they did not do, Maria Theresa in particular did not do it. She did not abandon the hope that she might yet get Silesia back, despite the Peace of Aix; and that is a black mark against the name of that splendid, simple, high-hearted woman, who was

151

otherwise so deserving of all the interest and sympathy she got from Europe. But why was it that Europe — or its courts and governments — never felt easy on the score of this king? Because of the great mistrust, with which our story began, and which the King repaid with interest. The mistrust was rooted in his fundamentally strange, enigmatic character. Europe knew it to be a danger; and its later manifestations kept her constantly holding her breath.

The fact was that of all the powers who had gone to war over the Pragmatic Sanction, Frederick alone had gained something, had even gained a great deal. That he kept the splendid province was the least of his gains. But this beggarly young Prussia, with its poor two million souls, had measured itself beside, or against, Austria, as an equal; it had squeezed in among the great powers of Europe, and claimed to speak in all their counsels as one of them; it had forced them to reckon with Prussia as a political factor not merely weighty, but even decisive — for Frederick had managed to stage himself in the popular imagination as the balance-wheel of European equilibrium, at least so far as the relations between France and Austria were concerned. Now, it is very hard on Europe to be forced to change its attitude like that. It takes her centuries. She struggles, she scolds, she sneers; she denies the new factor any political, cultural, above all any moral justification, she cannot utter enough spite and venom against the newcomer, she sees nothing but a speedy ruin in store for him; and, if her prophecies do not look like fulfilling themselves with measurable haste, then all the old-established society of states are ready to bury the hatchet of their private quarrels over prestige and interests, however vital, in order to fall on the kill-joy and crush him. She will do that, or try to, twice, if need be, within a hundred and fifty years. Simple people like Frederick's philosopher friend Jordan, even in the second Silesian war, can never understand why it is that " the accounts in the newspapers are never favourable to us." Yes, it was strange. But the newspaper accounts could not prevent Frederick from keeping Silesia. And now, at least, with the guarantee safe in his pocket, surely he is satiated and satisfied? Apart from measures taken against him — was he, on his side, well and peacefully minded?

He did not give the impression that he meant to disarm immediately. He kept his army, after the Peace at Dresden, on a footing of a hundred and forty thousand men; there were in addition the " supernumerary troops," whose strength he doubled, so that he had at his disposition a trained reserve of sixteen thousand men. That made a hundred and fifty-six thousand " moustaches," an absurd figure for a country of Prussia's relative rank and economic resources. Louis XV had not so many soldiers, certainly not so many beastly good ones. For Frederick's army, out of all compass as far as numbers went, was put through its paces in a way that was the talk of Europe.

He made demands, and insisted on performance, with respect to mobility and tactical precision, unheard of in his time. The foreign military gentry who were allowed now and then to look on were amazed — and, even so, they did not get to see the real thing. These masses of troops wheeled and deployed, they developed the famous oblique battle-order, invented by the King, in eight various formations, with a mathematical accuracy that would have made old Prince Eugene, who had once patronized the Prince at Philippsburg, doubt his own eyes. And there reigned throughout a practical spirit which was quite the opposite of amateurish enthusiasm. There were no splendid encampments and display manœuvres, as in other countries, where huge assemblages of troops came together in time of peace and went harmlessly through their exercises. Frederick held manœuvres on a large scale each year at Spandau or Potsdam; and these forced advances over heavy ground, these actions on the plain, these river crossings and assaults, these varied and whole-hearted attacks on the problem of how a superior enemy — it seemed one reckoned with a superior enemy, possibly with a combination of enemies? — can be rolled up on the flank and destroyed; they were all trials of war, in bitter earnest and quite undisguised, carried out with the sole end and aim of visualizing the actual conflict and familiarizing officers and troops with the details of the bloody business. And an aggressive spirit, a purpose of swift and lively action, was inoculated by every possible means into the blood of these troops — contrary to the fashion of the time and bordering on the uncivilized. Frederick had only contempt for the refined methods of making war as practised in his century — those " capital generals, who have spent whole campaigns in various manœuvres, without one being able to get the better of the other — which earned them high praise from the General Staff." He despised too the entrenched position, which was held in such great regard. Battle, at all costs! Force the enemy to fight; battles must be decisive, that is what they are for. Attack, attack! *Attaquez donc toujours!* A bayonet charge is his passion, he was the first to regulate the details of its execution. " Don't shoot more than you need, and, above all, not too soon! At twenty, even ten paces from the enemy, let off a good stiff salvo under his nose and then give it him in the ribs with the bayonet." Then the cavalry: " The King herewith forbids all officers of cavalry, on pain of disgrace and cassation, ever to let themselves be attacked in any action; for Prussians must always attack the enemy." At a hand-gallop? No, in full career. " Then, in close formation, they must spur their horses on, at the top of their lungs, as they charge." " At the top of their lungs." " Under their noses." " Give it them in the ribs." It all sounds so savage, so reckless, so extreme, so inordinate, so violent! The man must be bent on a ruthless offensive and thinking of nothing else. Is it possible for anyone to trust him?

Alas, no, probably not. Probably it was not possible, even if anyone had wanted to — again, quite apart from any measures taken against him! This king was much too secretive and dissembling; reserved even with his intimates, or, rather, he had no intimates. Never to be communicative, never to let anyone guess his thoughts, such was his first principle as a ruler. He stated it quite frankly one day, himself: " If I thought," he said, " that my shirt or my

155

skin knew anything of my intentions, I would tear them off." A savage way of putting it — and very expressive of his extreme and obstinate intention to keep his own counsel. What could be accomplished by diplomatic methods, with such a king? The foreign gentlemen found him inscrutable. His moderation, his neutrality, his good intentions — nobody believed in them, and he knew that they did not. He said: " In Vienna they take me for an irreconcilable enemy of the house of Austria; in London they think me far more restless, more ambitious, richer than I am. Bestuchev [the Russian imperial chancellor] believes that I am plotting mischief; in Versailles they say I am falling asleep over my interests. They are all mistaken. But what makes for trouble is that these misapprehensions may have evil consequences. What must be done is to anticipate [?] these consequences, and relieve Europe of her preconception." *Pre*-conception? Why, it was a *post*-conception, a conception formed after the two Silesian wars. Again, perhaps he was speaking quite sincerely, and merely deceived himself on the score of the danger he himself was to Europe? A puzzle to everybody, was he perhaps one to himself as well?

He led a singular life — it contrasted with any and every monarchical habit of the time. In summer he got up at three o'clock. But three o'clock is the time to go to bed, when God has placed you in a position to enjoy life! Scarcely was his hair combed when he began to govern. Did he govern well? Certainly he governed with a suspiciousness, a self-will, a despotism which could only be called boundless and extravagant, and which entered into everything, the smallest as well as the greatest field, and deprived the work of others of all dignity. He so loved work that he took it all to himself, and left his servants not enough; or, rather, what remained was irksome and petty, and he spied on and scolded and humiliated them even at that. " *Cette race maudite* " (thus, rightly or wrongly, he called the whole of humanity) would, he was convinced, begin to deceive him and defraud the State if it got the least chance; and his complete lack of confidence had at least this much good about it, that his officials had to reckon with the fact that the King would see and examine everything, his subjects might be certain that their complaints and petitions did come before him instead of falling under the table. He never let anything be lost sight of, he gave himself pain over the smallest detail.

Yes, self-willed and despotic he certainly was; up to the most grandiose and down to the pettiest sense of those words. Nobody dared travel without his permission; in granting which, the King decreed the amount of the journey money, down to a farthing: for the burgher so much, for the junker a little more. He awed and astonished all the world by operations that had something superhuman and fantastic about them, such as erecting mighty dams to fight the power of the sea and to wrench from it strips of land which had for centuries been its prey. Or he ploughed the marshes, turned bogs into fields, set ten thousand spades to work to make canals through the swamps of the Oderbruch — callous toward the suffering of his labourers, who might

157

all die off of swamp-fever, so long as they were sacrificed to the future and to his impatient will. If a stranger wanted a good seat at a parade, he had to write to the King, and the King answered in his own hand. Yet it was this very king who one day declared that he would no longer sit silent and endure the obsolete abuses and formalities in the administration of justice; he would mix in and attack the problem himself — and straightway he created the common law of the land, a great and bold reform, a model of reason and fair-mindedness, which all other countries were fain to study and admire.

The army, the administration, service at home and abroad. That was not all. He " mixed into " other matters too, and did not stop with " mixing." He was his own finance minister (obstinately stingy here; extravagant there, where it was a matter of some large and it might be impossible scheme or other), his own minister for agriculture (who simply refused to believe, because Linnæus and others said so, that the potato was a poisonous plant, and arbitrarily insisted that it be planted), his own minister for commerce (and as such conservative, walking in his father's footsteps, with prohibited schedules and protection and monopolies, his main idea being that the money should stop in the country), his own minister of works and mines, his own lord chamberlain, and what not besides? — for when a man lives separated from his wife and gets up at three o'clock in the morning, he can get a lot done in the course of the day.

It took a king like this, a man who could work as he

could, to show the full meaning of the word " despotism."
Until his time no one had grasped its significance. But the
despotism he created was a new kind. He was an enlightened despot — which means that his subjects might think
and say what they liked, provided that he, on his side,
might do as he chose — an arrangement which it must be
admitted was useful to both parties. Religions meant little
or nothing to him, he despised them all. Persecuted ir-
religion found an asylum and even an official status in his
kingdom. Lampoons, satires, libels directed against him,
moved him not at all. He did not fear brains: his love of
them was balanced by his scorn — so long as they were
not backed by any power. On being told that one of his subjects had criticized him, he asked: "Has he a hundred
thousand men? Then what do you want me to do with him? "
Which was cynical, of course. And, indeed, he did have
a cynical cast of mind, which betrayed itself even in his
dress, that got dirtier and shabbier as time went on; and
in the kind of diversions he chose: the habitual blasphemies
at his supper parties, the dry, malicious pleasure he had
in goading on the literary men and philosophers whom he
found in food, in " embroiling " them in disputes and
quarrels with each other. Even his mania for work, was
there not something cynical, arid, inhuman, misanthropic,
about it too, to any healthy and right human sense? For a
healthy and right human sense understands — and understood in Frederick's time too — that career and accom-
plishment are not all of life; that life has its purely human
claims and duties of happiness, to neglect which may be

a greater sin than a little easy-goingness toward oneself and others in the matter of one's work; and again, according to the healthy and right human sense, nobody can be called a harmonious personality who does not understand how to satisfy the just claims of both sides of life. And this king did not, he had no comprehension of these facts, though surely a king ought to know them as well as other people. His insane industry, his insistence on merit and getting things done, was ascetic and somehow horrible in its nature. He hated monks, of course, as he hated all religious and clergy; but he was rather like a monk himself, a monk in a blue soldier coat and yellow waistcoat always spotted with snuff. And he was a cynical old bachelor, and a good share of his ill feeling and his uncanniness had surely to do with his relations with the female sex, which were as a matter of fact no relations at all, and pretty incomprehensible even to his own age, highly capricious as that was in its attitude toward sex matters.

He had been, as I said, rather a dissipated youth. When he was fifteen years old, he visited the luxurious court of Dresden, where he liked it not a little, and fell in love head over ears with the Countess Orselska, the daughter and favourite of Augustus II; but the King, who was somewhat jealous, offered him instead the Countess Formera, a well-shaped damsel, displaying her first in the guise of a living picture. This lady accordingly became Frederick's first mistress. Afterwards he got hold of the Orselska as well. Such tales are legion: for instance, there is one about the Freifrau von Wreech, whom he used to visit when he was at Küstrin, and who supplied him with candles and books, and even with money, which he is supposed never to have refunded, though Frau von Wreech gave birth to a child which her husband never acknowledged. Then there was the daughter of a Potsdam precentor, who was publicly whipped and sent to the house of correction " for life." And in Ruppin and Rheinsberg he had his fill of debauchery; but Seckendorff wrote to Prince Eugene that " it seemed the body was not strong enough for the demands made upon it by the desires, and the Crown Prince appears to seek in his dissipations a reputation for gallantry rather than to gratify actual sinful inclinations." All which might be true and might not. But it is certain that none of these affairs had anything to do with passion in any higher or deeper sense, any more than they had with genuine feeling or warmth of heart. Frederick, when quite young, declared that all he wanted of women was pleasure, and that, having enjoyed, he despised them. He had never been in love. Then came a *malheur;* there is talk of an operation following; and from then on something was broken in his nature. He soon ceased to act the voluptuary; woman had played out her brief and not too honourable rôle in his life.

Misogyny is now deep-seated in his nature. Henceforth one cannot imagine him in any tender situation — it would seem grotesque. His marriage, of course, was no marriage at all; but that does not signify, since it was a forced one. It was not merely that the other sex left him cold. He hated it, he poured scorn on it, he could not endure it anywhere

161

near him. His wife's ladies complained: "We do not ask that the King should love us; but that he simply cannot stand us — that is hard." The wife of his hypochondriac friend d'Argens was allowed, as a particular favour, to live in Sans Souci; save for this the palace was a sort of cloister. But a cloister is not quite a natural place to live in. The Italian dancer Barberini passed for some time as the King's mistress; but Voltaire, on the subject of the relationship, expressed himself thus: " *Il en était un peu amoureux parce qu'elle avait les jambes d'un homme.*" So it too was hardly the regular thing. Frederick's masculinity was obviously not attracted in the orthodox way by the feminine counter-pole. Possibly the long years of soldiering contributed to this state of things and weaned his interests from the other sex. There are many cases of military who were or who became women-haters. This man, brought up in an atmosphere of French femininity, may have grown so accustomed to the maleness of camps that at last he " could not stand the smell " of women. And this was in the Frenchest of centuries, a woman's century *par excellence,* saturated with the perfume of the *Ewig-Weibliche.* His conception of soldiership, ascetic to begin with (the highest soldier in his command durst not in the field eat off anything but tin), made him so anti-feminine that the soft appeal of love and marriage was quite shut out. He did not like his officers' marrying, he wanted them to be cloistered warriors like himself; and expressed his view in the witticism he made, that his officers " should find their happiness in the sword and not in the . . ." Anyhow, they should find it in

162

the sword. In 1778, out of the seventy-four officers of a regiment of dragoons there was just one married.

Now why was all that? Perhaps at bottom it was not a little political. We must not forget that the most powerful countries in Europe were at that time ruled by women: the Empress Elizabeth, the Empress-queen of Austria, and the Pompadour. Frederick despised and affronted them to the point of political gaucherie. Aloud, at table, before all his lackeys, he called them " the three first wh...s in Europe." This though he knew, or, rather, because he knew, that no remark of his escaped the spies of foreign courts. In any case, the ugly word may have fitted two of them, but certainly it did not Maria Theresa; in vituperating that chaste and childishly high-minded woman he obviously only levelled at the sex. The Little Mother, Elizabeth, on the other hand, did lay herself open by her weakness for strong drink and muscular military; but these very weaknesses were what kept her a powerful potentate, and it was most injudicious of Frederick to make them the theme of scurrilous little rhymes, which of course came to her ears and made the mistress of Russia his envenomed and everlasting enemy. And why could he not bring himself to the point of a few friendly words with the Pompadour, after she had daintily taken pains to meet him half-way — and considering she was the actual ruler of France? She was only a butcher's daughter, named Poisson, the wife of a publican and procurer, and herself a procuress to boot. Admitted and conceded, that was what she was. But in the first place, what is the good of being an enlightened despot if you cannot look beyond such small matters? And in the second, she was rather more than delicious, with that clever, roguish little head and that billowing embroidered frock — its measured décolletage sagely half-hiding, half-revealing delights which an all-Christian king had known how to value. Scarcely a sign betrayed the filth whence she came and which remained her element. She knew how to preside discreetly over a privy council. Frederick, when he wantonly repulsed her, was aiming at the female rather than at the concubine. " I do not know her," he said: " *Je ne la connais pas.*" Anybody else, in his place, would have rued that, later. Maria Theresa — foundress of the chastity commission, pious and faithful wife — displayed more self-control. " *Princesse et Cousine,*" she wrote; " *Madame ma très chère Sœur* " — it sounds scandalous, but it had to be done, for Silesia's sake. As for Frederick's bearing toward the Empress-queen herself, it sets in the clearest light his callousness where the sex was concerned. All the chroniclers and critics, chivalrous before everything else, speak of his behaviour as abominable.

There is a beautiful portrait drawing of the Empress-queen, by Meytens, in the copperplate collection in Berlin. There is the sumptuous rococo head, majestic and sturdy at once, proud and naïve: the pure brow, with a little diadem above it crowning the powdered hair that falls in curls upon the royal shoulders. There is the double chin, childishly dignified, the clear eyes, the powerful hooked nose, the wholesome mouth, full without being coarse. Her voice is said to have had a compelling charm. Court and

164

people idolized her. She reigned in the fear of God, piously, patriarchally, comfortably. To her husband, Franz of Lorraine, a famous petticoat-chaser, she was a loyal wedded wife, conniving at all his shortcomings. When he died, she turned to his sobbing mistress, Princess Auersperg, and said: " My dear Princess, we have both lost much." She was as good-natured as that. When her son, Duke Leopold of Tuscany, made her a grandmother for the first time, she was so beside herself for joy that she ran in her night-dress through the castle corridors to the Burgtheater, where there was a performance. Leaning out over the balcony of the royal box she called down into the house: " Poldy's got a baby! And, to cap the climax, on my wedding-anniversary! Isn't he a love? " We hear her call, we share the rapture of her audience. She was not yet four-and-twenty when her father died and bequeathed her the burden of the crown. Her health tottered beneath the defeat of Mollwitz and the ensuing crisis; for, to add to everything else, she was with child. " For all my realms were the field of battle," she later wrote, " and I knew not where I could be brought to bed in peace." Yet with what lofty spirit, what touching courage, she bore herself! Still weak from her lying-in, on her arm the infant whom in tears and troubles she had brought into the world, the crown of Saint Stephen on her head, she stood in Pressburg before the assembly of the Empire and summoned the chivalry of her Hungary to the defence of her insulted majesty. And the magnates — one can see them — in frenzied enthusiasm swung their crooked sabres and pressed round the throne with the cry: " We will

165

die for our King, Maria Theresa!" But Frederick was without bowels of feeling for this majestic weakness; probably the pale maternity of his enemy only added fuel to the flames of his masculinity, and rather roused disgust than reverence. Throughout the long, inhuman struggle to which the two Silesian wars were the prelude, the thought that he was dealing with women never left him a moment. It recurs in countless of his utterances of that time; who knows if the shameful thought of being defeated by three women was not what stiffened his back? At the thanksgiving service after the victory of Mollwitz he gave out the text from I Timothy ii. 12: "But I suffer not a woman to teach, nor to usurp authority over the man, but to be silent." — Maria Theresa, when she heard about it, was not a little wroth. She had a name for him, at once childish and oracular; it seems to show that her woman's intuition pierced the secret of his character. She never named him save as "the bad man." The bad man. Yes, that he was, with the emphasis as much on man as on bad. The mysteries of sex are very profound, never will they be quite explained. Was it that this king could not endure women because he was such a bad man, or that he was such a bad man because he could not endure women? A riddle not to be unriddled. But that the two things were somehow dependent on each other — of that I feel certain.

"The bad man": he was that to everybody, though it was Maria Theresa who by preference and from the depths of her heart gave him the name. There was always a whispering and a plotting and a conspiring round about him — defensively, of course, in the end, and as precautionary measures — all directed against him; he had always to realize it, even when he knew nothing specific; and he parried, as well as he could, ten years long. Yes, we must agree that during all that time he was, diplomatically speaking, on the defensive against his worse nature — though one might, indeed, get the impression that even this behaviour was dictated by sheer malice and in order to lead honest people by the nose. . . . To sum up, the constellation of great powers was at that time as follows:

The traditional, three-hundred-year-old rivalry between France and Austria was a settled factor, a political constant, which it seemed would have to be reckoned with to all eternity. It had brought France and Prussia together and the alliance of June 1744 had still up to '56 to run. But that alliance had become rather loose and unreliable, after Frederick withdrew — prematurely, in the view of France — from the War of the Succession. As for England, her hostility toward France was if possible even more venerable than that country's toward Austria. France loomed large upon the continent, France had a fleet, overseas interests (there were disputes in America, more precisely in Canada) — in short, quite enough to make England keep a sharp eye on her. And George II could endure Frederick as little as anybody else. He too, though not a female, had been satirized in an epigram. And so England clave to Russia, where the amateur of strong drink and muscular soldiers sat enthroned; and did this with especial reference to Prussia; Prussia being still regarded as an ally of France,

167

and in a position, in case of war between the latter and the English, to attack England on her continental heel of Achilles — in other words, Hanover. . . . The attitude of Saxon Poland was particularly curious, involved, and timid — under an Augustus anything but Strong, or, rather, under his prime minister and head of the Cabinet, Count Brühl, a great spender, a great roué and intriguer, who presently ruined the country financially and after that politically too. This man possessed two hundred pairs of shoes, eight hundred embroidered night-shirts, five hundred suits of clothes, one hundred and two watches, eight hundred and forty-three tobacco-boxes, eighty-seven rings, fifty-seven smelling-bottles, twenty-nine coaches, and fifteen hundred wigs. But I digress. — On Sweden Frederick thought he could count, his sister Ulrike being crown princess there. French influence, also, was paramount in that country — that is, it drew subsidies from France.

The intrigues, the war of pens and plottings against a greater Prussia, began, so to speak, while the ink was still wet on the signatures to the Peace of Dresden. Next to Austria, where the alienation of Silesia was regarded as entirely temporary, the chief source of the intrigues was Russia; Austria, of course, always played the rôle of diplomat with a light touch, whereas Russia, at all times clumsy, at all times ready to conspire, hammered away at the war and the annexation of East Prussia. I mentioned that Russia's leader of foreign affairs was Bestuchev, the imperial chancellor, who took care, by arrangement with the Austrian and English agents, to feed the alcoholic

168

hatred of his mistress for the King of Prussia, and to hold the resources of his half-savage country at the service of Austria. Scarcely any relations now subsisted between the courts of Berlin and Saint Petersburg. A sort of latent state of war obtained. Every spring, troops assembled in the Baltic Provinces and threatened to overflow the Prussian border. But there had to be some show of conducting matters in the European way; so all sorts of documents were drawn up on parchment, with secret clauses and everything proper and in order.

The fact was that as early as 1745 an alliance had been entered into by the maritime powers and the Saxon-Polish and Hungarian courts — the famous Warsaw Alliance, so-called. It had only been ratified in the spring of that year, at Leipsic, and looked harmless enough on the surface, but it had a secret clause, the Warsaw Agreement, signed only by the monarchs of Hungary and Poland, which was definitely directed against the robber of Silesia. Scarcely had the Peace of Dresden been signed, when Vienna, through the proper diplomatic channels, let it be known in Dresden that she hoped the Warsaw Agreement was still in force. Brühl would have been delighted to utter a hearty yes in reply; but that he was afraid to; began to wriggle, and through all the following years continued to wriggle, until the arrival of the catastrophe. Saxony had come off unharmed from the Peace of Dresden; contrary to her expectations, for when Frederick was fighting in Bohemia she had attacked him in the rear. But he contented himself with an indemnity — the victor of Soor and

Kesselsdorf was just then behaving with great moderation, not to say magnanimity. Brühl, however, hated Frederick; at that time everything political had a strong personal coloration, and the hatred of the luxurious and effeminate minister-president toward the ascetic and industrious soldier was inborn and indestructible, it yielded nothing in violence to the Austrian brand. Brühl would have been delighted to give it free vent; but there was the outward attitude of Saxony toward the Prussian states, and there was the abominable superiority of the Prussian army. " The Warsaw Agreement," answered Brühl: yes, it subsisted, and then again, it did not subsist. It subsisted conditionally. It subsisted on condition that it did no harm to Saxony. It subsisted on condition that Russia joined it. It was indispensable that Russia should join — if she did, then by all means. It went without saying. " *Parfaitement*," replied Austria, and applied to Russia; and Russia barely waited to be asked, she was on the spot at once, with clumsy and unlimited zeal. In the year '46 a defensive alliance — only defensive, of course — was arranged between Austria and Russia. It contained a secret clause, to the effect that if the King attacked either of them, he should be held to have forfeited Silesia thereby — beloved, lamented Silesia, which grew dearer and dearer to the Empress-queen, the more she saw what Frederick knew how to get out of it; Catholic Silesia, whose possession by a heretic and criminal cried to heaven. Brühl was politely invited to come in . . . but Brühl still wriggled. No, no signature, no official commitment, it was too dangerous. And as they were sure of his

170

good intentions, they let him off the signature, in God's name. If anybody accuses Saxony of having joined an alliance against Frederick, he lies. Saxony had preserved its neutrality, Saxony had not signed. That it had done its utmost, with Austria, to stir up trouble in Saint Petersburg is another matter. It was neutral, none the less; it had not signed.

A defensive alliance, be it known, is an alliance which only begins to be in force when one or another party to it is attacked by a given other power or group of powers. But one speaks in strategy of an offensive defensive; and it would appear that something of the kind may also occur in the diplomatic sphere; indeed, if it were not for the conciliatory title, it might sometimes be very hard to distinguish a defensive alliance from its reprehensible opposite. In politics, as also in life, the name is mostly a sort of *concession au publique*, and deals only superficially with the fact it represents. An attack may be of sheer necessity; but then it is not an attack at all, it is a defence. And if an attack is advantageous to the members of the defensive alliance, why, then it becomes as good as impossible to draw the psychological line where the *casus fœderis* ceases to be a contingency which everybody would unite in avoiding, and turns into something devoutly to be wished. Thus it becomes a question of sensibility, and has to be left to the feeling of the allies, when one of them shall and will feel itself attacked; and accordingly, to invoke the *casus fœderis* it is only necessary to drive your opponent to do the attacking — in other words, to force him into the rôle of formal

171

aggressor, which is scarcely very difficult, and may be, under some circumstances, very easy. Things will inevitably so shape themselves, when one of the parties to the defensive alliance is a power like the Muscovite kingdom, a power whose instinct to expand has something elemental and irresponsible about it, like the stretching and the appetite of a giant; a power which, knowing itself ultimately unconquerable, is at all times clumsily eager for the fray. Now, as for this defensive alliance between Austria and Russia, aimed at Prussia: the Empress Maria Theresa had repeatedly and solemnly renounced Silesia, and she was much too god-fearing a woman even to think of breaking the compacts of Dresden, Breslau, and Aix-la-Chapelle. But for that very reason she needed to find a way of getting back Silesia which should be morally possible; and this she secured by the alliance with Russia. For if Frederick were to attack, he would lose his right to the province. Which was now for the good Maria Theresa the *casus fœderis* — a danger or a desirability? Let us call it a tempting danger, or a troubling desire. But what Russia understood by the word " defensive " is clear from the fact that in 1753 it was formally announced in the council of state in Saint Petersburg, and made the basis of a protocol, that it would also be permissible to attack Prussia in case an ally of Russia attacked her first. A corollary perhaps rather alcoholic in origin, but it makes the question wherein a defensive alliance differs, except in name, from another, to a certain extent legitimate.

Well, and did Frederick know of these things? Oh, yes,

172

one thing and another did come to his ears in the course of these years, if more by way of a trickle than in a steady stream. He had to put them together and make sense of them himself. The system of espionage was just then at the height of its flower, blossoming rather more luxuriantly than it does today; and Frederick was its greatest supporter, considering it to be of the highest importance to maintain spies everywhere, in all the important places. He called them his "*Kujons*" (rascals) or "*Pfaffen*" (parsons), and never could have too many of them — especially since they did not cost very much. Brühl had set up a whole office in Dresden just for deciphering the Prussian dispatches; so we may consider it in the light of a retort on Frederick's part that he kept a "*Kujon*" there in his pay, to post him in events important for the King to know. This famous *filou*, named Menzel, a book-keeper by occupation, had access to the files which contained the secret documents of the government of Saxony, and for years made copies of the diplomatic correspondence between Russia and Vienna, which, together with the replies sent by the wriggling Brühl, he punctually dispatched to Potsdam. From these documents Frederick gleaned precisely the dealings which Saxony had with Vienna and Saint Petersburg at the beginning and toward the middle of the fifties. He learned how Brühl wriggled and twisted in order both to preserve and to betray the neutrality of Saxony; how Russia was persuaded to come in; how they egged her on, in her clumsy enthusiasm, to bring things to a point; how a god-fearing empress set to work to find a valid, an ethical excuse for action. He learned

173

— if he had not known before — what sort of thing a defensive alliance might be, when directed against himself; and, supposing that he, on his side, was not god-fearing and peaceably disposed, not at all inclined to rest on the laurels of Hohenfriedberg, but, on the contrary, cherishing all sorts of schemes and treacheries — then, here in these very papers, he himself possessed the moral possibility which the good Empress-queen was to reap from his offensive. As you see, the real inwardness of things was somewhat complicated, though it was, on Frederick's side, more downright, more contemptuous, less involved, than it was with Maria Theresa and the man who, as Frederick said, had fifteen hundred wigs and no head.

I pass over the numerous provocations, intrigues, and crises of the second class, which occupied the political world during these years of peace, without lying on the direct line of the march of events. As early as the spring of '49, the eager Bestuchev had come very near to springing the mine — on the score of the antagonism between France and England. The Duke of Newcastle, then the head of the English Foreign Office, was working for an alliance directed against France, which should include, besides the sea powers, Russia, Austria, Saxony, and a few other German states — all very much to Bestuchev's mind, for here the prospect beckoned him of involving Sweden and Prussia in a general conflict. He set to work in Sweden, where he thought to bring about a change in the succession, and wean the country from French and Prussian influence, drawing it within the sphere of Russian control. He hoped in this way to force Prussia to act in a military sense. And when he demanded from England, Austria, and Saxony a declaration that he might count on their support in his Swedish undertakings, the whole world expected an immediate catastrophe. But Frederick maliciously drew his neck out of the noose. He invoked the French interest in behalf of Sweden, he mildly warned the London uncle; and as he gave emphasis to his diplomacy by calling up his reserves, England and Austria found it expedient to dissociate themselves from Russia. Moreover, Denmark was won over to the Prussian-Swedish-French *entente;* there was even talk that Turkey would come in. In short, the hostile combination was sprung, Bestuchev was isolated and obliged to put off the execution of his plans to a better time.

But the initiative now passed to an Austrian statesman, with a name famous in history, who at this stage of developments stepped full length into the picture: lean and stiff, in a peruke powdered with excessive care, the curls of which were arranged to hide the wrinkles on his forehead; with a long, calm, blue-eyed, almost English face, and a huge diamond order in his velvet coat. His name was Kaunitz, Wenzel Anton Count Kaunitz; Maria Theresa, who early recognized his great talents, later made him a prince. He was an oddity, such as the eighteenth century brought forth in numbers. Excessively hypochondriac — another peculiarity fashionable in that time — he abominated fresh air, and never went out of doors, so that he was as white as a cellar plant. In his pocket he carried a whole little arsenal of dental instruments, which he brought out after a meal — even when he dined out — and began to rummage about in his mouth with a lot of rags and lancets and little mirrors. Until one time the French ambassador said: *"Levons-nous; le prince veut être seul."* After that Kaunitz left off going into society. Goodness knows how many other maggots he had in his brain; but as a politician he was shrewd, far-sighted, judicial, and with an enormous gift for sticking to a plan once formed. And he had just one thought in his head: Prussia must be thrown by the heels, if the illustrious house of Austria were to continue in existence. That was a good and right thought, from his point of view, but it had in itself nothing original about it. What was original, original and really magnificent, was the method which Kaunitz, and Kaunitz alone, evolved in order to put his thought into execution.

Kaunitz comprehended that to checkmate Prussia and crowd her to the wall it was necessary not only to break up the Franco-Prussian alliance, but actually to draw France over to the Austrian side. If genius consists in essential independence of thought, that was a conception worthy of the name. All the world over, it was an impossible idea that France and Austria should ever walk hand in hand. Sooner would fire and water mix. The mutual jealousy of the two houses had left its mark on the whole history of Europe — not merely since the days of the great Richelieu. But, granted that this was so, Kaunitz could not see why it should be so for ever. " Much is not dared " — so ran his device — " Much is not dared because it seems hard, much seems hard only because it is not dared." He acted upon this motto. If France decided to join the Saint Petersburg offensive-and-defensive alliance, she brought Sweden over with her; Saxony too would not hesitate to turn on Frederick, so soon as she risked nothing by the act; and if the Versailles government no longer stirred up the German princes against the house of Austria, the German states were pretty certain to be loyal. By a general understanding such as that, everybody stood to win. If France were instrumental in the recovery of Silesia, she would be allowed as a reward some enlargement in Flanders. East Prussia would fall to Russia, Magdeburg to Saxon Poland; if Sweden cared in the least about Pomerania, she would be a fool to stand aside. Anyhow, Sweden had no choice, she was bound by French money. If hope and hatred once moved them all to strike this monstrous alliance, then Frederick was surrounded, hopelessly and helplessly, and a coalition formed such as the world had never seen before: a glorious coalition, which history could not but christen with the name of Wenzel Anton Kaunitz.

These ideas did not spring full-grown in one day from the head of their originator. Like all good things they had deep beginnings. Even at the Peace of Aix-la-Chapelle, which Kaunitz concluded for Austria, he offered Brabant and Flanders to Versailles, on condition that his country recovered Silesia by means of French assistance. But France declined. Considering her position with regard to England, she found the Prussian alliance too valuable to be weakened by such undertakings. Since that date Kaunitz had industriously fed and fostered the mistrust of the bad man at

Potsdam in all the courts of Europe. From 1747 to 1748 he was consul in London, where he plied George II with intercepted Prussian dispatches and a thousand insinuations against his nephew. But in the year 1751 he came to Paris, and there began the golden age of his career as an intriguer.

He lived in the Palais Bourbon like a private gentleman of quality, with several women whom he gave entertainment; but he received very little. However, with the two important persons, the monarch and the Poisson person, he was on the best of terms; it was he who brought his liege lady in Vienna to the point of those *princesse et cousine* letters which were probably the hardest sacrifice ever legitimacy laid upon the altar of politics. Kaunitz pursued his aims with a tact and persistence truly admirable. He knew that at bottom the Most Christian King, despite the alliance still in force, abominated Frederick. Louis was bigoted and lazy; coddled, self-indulgent, uxorious; naturally his active, soldierly, free-thinking, Protestant cousin of Brandenburg was an offence to him. The alliance existed for reasons of state, of course; it was directed against England, and threatened Hanover, the English possession on the continent. But as for personal or dynastic sympathies, they were nil, there was no basis for them; and setting the political aside, a friendship between two old, aristocratic houses like Bourbon and Habsburg was more humanly fitting than the one that obtained between Versailles and the upstart breed of the Potsdam drill-sergeant. And the creature had written scurrilous lampoons against our marquise, and government by mistresses, and our all-highest and laziest

178

Majesty's sacred person: Kaunitz hinted very skilfully, and now and then was in a position to produce a bit of new evidence. What audacity, what ingratitude this king displayed! What immemorial disloyalty! For never, unless with France's help, could he have got Silesia for himself, and how had he shown his gratitude? By leaving her in the lurch and crawling off into the woods with his prey. But that is the way little states always behave when the big ones fall out among themselves. To whose use and behoof, when you think of it, had France and Austria been at each others' throats all these centuries? *Cui bono?* — to speak Latin. Had either one of them gained anything? No, they had only weakened each other; the gainers had been the small and middle-sized states, who otherwise would have had to do as they were told, and who now were fishing in troubled waters. It was this Prussian land-grabber who had won; thanks to the discord between France and Austria, he had gained a position for which nature had not intended him. Kaunitz was not so radical as to assert that an understanding between his own country and France was conceivable, possible, perhaps even necessary. Only it was amusing to imagine how things would be if such an understanding were to come within the range of possibilities. It would be like heaven, that was all. Everybody's cares and troubles would vanish, you would wish for a thing and it would fall into your lap. Poor Silesia — it would not take long to wrench it from the clutches of the bad man. And if France also dreamed dreams — Flemish dreams — be sure Austria would find an opportunity to show herself grateful. What else? Nothing else, probably — save that, yes, France and Austria united would simply be able to do anything they wanted to. Strengthened on both sides, in splendid equilibrium, without occasion for jealousy, they would hold sway in Europe, and every foreign will would have to bow the knee in face of their united front. So would it be if a concord between them were possible. But such was not the case; unfortunately, not at all. Tradition compelled them to work against each other, to the end that neither of them got anything; and so it must be, to all eternity. Habits were strong, bad habits were the strongest. Stronger than all else was prejudice, and reason must bow before it. — Or must it?

This was the sort of thing that Kaunitz dropped into every ear which stayed still long enough to listen. He trotted out his theory on every occasion, turned it this side and that, showed it in various lights. First people laughed, then they stopped to think. It was daring, it was amusing — after a while they wondered if perhaps it might not be more than a joke. Gradually it became the *dernier cri*, a political mode, *très chic* as a topic of conversation in boudoirs and coffee-houses. The erstwhile Poisson was enchanted with it — and the Empress had written her such a charming letter! But there were sound ministerial reasons for not repudiating the alliance with Prussia; and Kaunitz's paradoxes could not so soon have taken on even a half-way tangible form, had not the man against whom they were directed advantaged all his labours.

Frederick probably felt that a cooler breeze had begun

180

to blow from Versailles; and the French attitude seemed the more foolish to him in that an English-French conflict was looming large and black on the horizon. They would surely come to blows on the subject of the French-Canadian border-line; the rivalry of the two maritime powers was pressing to a warlike issue; and as Frederick's treaty with France could not possibly extend to a Prussian guarantee of the French possessions in America, he felt that France might reasonably be solicitous about his friendship. What was it Versailles wanted? If it was a land war, if it wanted to attack England in Hanover, then surely Prussia's help was more important than this new flirtation with Vienna — a joke which would soon be played out when the war with England was once on. For ever since the days of Louis XIV Austria's place, and Holland's too, had been on the English side in a French and English war. And as for Russia, England did not spare her guineas when she set out to bribe the Muscovite navy " against the common foe." And the common foe — Frederick might flatter himself that he was the man. England had in him a not quite comfortable neighbour on the continent, and she did well to take precautions against a Prussian attack on her electorate of Hanover. But while she set her diplomacy to work, what did France do? France did nothing at all, whereas there were three things at least which she should have done. She should have stirred up Turkey, to hold the two empires in check. She should have come to an understanding with Frederick on the subject of Hanover. And, lastly, she should have brought England to hear reason, by attacking Hanover.

Frederick had been expecting for months that the Duke of Nivernais would come to Potsdam to negotiate. But he did not come. Obviously, Kaunitz was at the bottom of that. Frederick thought the petticoat government at Versailles was showing itself pitiably hare-brained and silly. England was sending a fleet to America; she was capturing French ships and King George was threatening in parliament; but Louis and his one-time Poisson seemed bent on repose. The only step Louis took was to instruct his foreign minister, Rouillé, to make the following proposal to the Prussian ambassador: "Write to your sovereign that he ought to assist us against Hanover. There will be a lot of plunder. The King of England's treasury is well filled. The King need only help himself." It was brazen. But it shows incidentally what sort of repute King Frederick enjoyed in Europe and particularly at the court of Versailles. He sent back the reply that if they had proposals like that to make they would do better to employ a Mandrin as go-between (Mandrin being a notorious highway robber). He hoped that in future M. Rouillé would make a distinction between the persons with whom he had to deal. A haughty, virtuous answer — and one that would certainly make a good impression in England.

Frederick had chosen between England and France. He saw the latter vacillating, feeble, lacking in confidence. And he felt that he was being undermined in Paris by Prince Kaunitz. He gave France up. He was convinced that if he attacked Hanover he would have England, Austria, and Russia against him. On the other hand, if he cast in his

182

lot with England, in the first place the French would not come to Germany, and in the second he would have the money-bags on his side in all future contingencies. An understanding with Russia would thereby be achieved, and who knew if it might not in the future be possible to prize Russia loose from Austria, and by thus isolating Maria Theresa wean her from her hope of regaining Silesia? Here was the reasoning that underlay Frederick's humourless retort to M. Rouillé. And England heard it. Could she win over Hanover's dangerous neighbour, and thus secure her continental communications for her naval war with France? England took steps. And soon the *rapprochement* came about. By the middle of January 1756 a convention was signed at Westminster, according to which Prussia and England vowed mutual peace and friendship, and, in particular, bound themselves to act to prevent any armed power from marching into or through Germany. That was all.

Really it was not much. England certainly had no intention of falling out with Russia and Austria on Frederick's account. And, on his side, Frederick perhaps did not believe that an understanding with England must necessarily mean a break with France. But France was beside herself. Yes, Kaunitz was right. This man was an out and out wretch. He openly put himself on the side of France's enemies. But they would show him. . . . They showed him. Kaunitz had meanwhile taken the helm of foreign affairs at Vienna and was represented at Paris through Count Starhemberg. He could at once report the most gratifying progress in his French enterprise. It was at this time that our marquise showed how well she could preside at a real council of state. In the boudoir of her château of Babiole there took place those very private negotiations between her, Count Starhemberg, and the Abbé Bernis, her protégé, which, on May the first, resulted in a contract of defence and neutrality between France and Austria: the Treaty of Versailles, which was the answer to the Convention of Westminster, and which, as a matter of fact, was so well seasoned that somebody called it a blank declaration of war for the Austrian chancellor. In it was the statement that France and Austria would stand together, that in case of need one of them would place twenty-four thousand men at the disposition of the other; and there were also included all sorts of things about subsidies to Austria. It was not set down that Austria would cede territory in the Netherlands to France as soon as Austria by France's help had got back Silesia; but they continually treated of it, and the Marquise so understood it.

And if it were only France that was outraged! But Russia was outraged too. " What? " Elizabeth cried; " have we taken so much money from England only to have her patronize this man who has made a mock of me all over Europe for the sake of a few harmless little fancies? " Russia turned her back on England. With furious haste she set herself to get into touch once more with France. Furiously she proffered Austria a plain and blunt offensive alliance against Prussia. They could hardly hold her back. Kaunitz, who had not quite yet got France where he wanted her,

184

had to preach patience to Saint Petersburg, and advise discretion, " lest the desperate King of Prussia fall on us prematurely."

So Frederick, then, had missed his reckoning altogether — granted, of course, that he had reckoned as the writers of the period (among whom he was one) say that he did. And granting that he had not known all the time, in his heart of hearts, that in one way or another he would one day have to prove the strength of his budding greatness before the whole of Europe, and had been ready for many a day to do it. Today it looks as though both alternatives were true: that he had war in his blood, but that, more out of spite than love of peace, he played the diplomatic game of balancing powers — just for the fun of leading destiny by the nose. At all events, the Convention of Westminster caused an incredible political upheaval; and any critic of the time might have said that this royal statesman was such a bungler that he had managed to unite against him all the sworn hereditary enemies of Europe. A new system of understandings arose: Austria did not stick to England against France, and Bourbon and Habsburg joined hands. Russia disregarded the subsidies contracted for with England the previous year; mad with rage, she went over to France and Austria. And so they were united, they, the three greatest powers on the continent. And on the other side stood Frederick; with a single friend, not exaggeratedly loyal at that, who concealed from him that she was no longer friends with Russia, and who, moreover, had her hands full with the war overseas. However, the famous

185

money-belt would be at his disposition, at least for the present and if things did not go too badly with him.

Such was the position; and it did not take Frederick long to grasp it. Not in vain did he keep spies at every court. He knew the secrets of Babiole. From The Hague came hints of the Franco-Russian *rapprochement.* " Are you sure of the Russians? " he continually asked Mitchell, the English ambassador. And Mitchell replied: " My government is sure of them." Adding *sotto voce* that he himself was not so sure, and that just lately a courier had told him that all the roads up to the Lithuanian frontier were full of marching Russians. For Mitchell the Scot was an honest man and he had great respect for Frederick. To make assurance doubly sure, word came from Dresden of Russia's eager urging, and of her leaving England in the lurch. The Viennese ambassador gave further detail about the offensive Austro-French alliance, which was not signed yet, but was under constant discussion; comprehensively speaking, it was as follows; on the day when Austria, with the help of France, won back Silesia, it ceded to France a part of the Netherlands. — Take it all in all, the Kaunitz schemes, his coalition and his dreams of partition, were pretty plain.

It was a great deal that Frederick had in his hands; quite enough to afford him the moral possibility which he was supposed to give the good Maria Theresa by attacking. It is not hard to guess his state of mind — to presume to understand his feelings would be more daring. A bitter, angry, Mephistophelian laughter must have risen to his lips

186

at the thought of that clique over there striving so hard to
preserve their innocence, to put on him the odium of the
offensive — on him, who was above either the simplicity
or the hypocrisy of such clear psychological distinctions
between offensive and defensive; and who had no fear of
either praise or blame. And again, he felt that Prussia
would have in the end to assert herself and show what she
could do; he had war in his blood, he meant war — whereas
the others only meant, in the first instance, diplomatic
chicanery. The draft of that Franco-Austrian alliance,
whose aim was the recovery of Silesia, presupposed an offensive taken by Frederick — and even so it remained a
draft. The whole Kaunitz scheme of a coalition for the
destruction of Prussia was in the first place no more than
that, and very little of it had been put on paper. There is no
document in existence from which Maria Theresa's intention to attack Prussia can be proved; nor any showing that
Russia's and Saxony's part in her plans was either a neutral
or a hostile one. No human being, learned or unlearned,
will ever be able to decide whether these plans would ever
have become more than plans if it had not been that. . . .
One thing more: a contemporary, who must have known,
Count Hertzberg, who at the King's request prepared a
paper upon the events of the year 1756 and preceding,
declared, thirty years later: " It is, to be sure, a fact that
plans were in existence for the partition of Frederick's
territories; but they were only provisional, and presupposed the condition that he would give occasion to carry
them out; so it will always remain unsettled whether or no

187

those plans would have been executed." If it had not been that — what? That Frederick himself began.

If one turns to the historians to try to discover whether the frightful war which thus began was really an offensive or a defensive war on Frederick's part, one finds that the historians contradict themselves to the point of absurdity. All those whose breasts are covered with orders have one song to sing; everything, they say, is against the libellous hypothesis of a long-prepared war of attack and conquest: the bearing of the King, his utterances, public and private, during the ten years of peace and the last summer months before the catastrophe. Those whose breasts are not covered with orders (which of course is only the result and not the cause of the views they hold), who have a grudge against genius, holding it to be incompatible with virtue, in the nature of things: these sing a different song: positively everything, they say, that is known to us of the villain speaks for the interpretation of an offensive war. His utterances, forsooth! They are just so many subterfuges, just so much dust in people's eyes. "If I thought my shirt or my skin knew anything of my intentions . . ." Yes, we remember. Had he not also said that he had no desire to be like those princes who become famous by reason of one brilliant operation and afterwards enjoy peace and quiet? His plans date from far back. He wanted to conquer Saxony and West Prussia, that was all, and he spied out the diplomacy of the other powers in order to get pretexts for attack. — Yes, the historians are a mass of contradictions. For my part, if anybody asks me, I prefer to say nothing. For it

188

seems to me that when the various opinions on his life and deeds cancel each other out, silence is what is left. That Frederick began the war is no evidence that it was not defensive; for he was encircled, and might quite possibly have been attacked the following spring. But did he will the war? The question leads us into the slough of unsolved problems concerning the freedom of the will. He probably understood quite early that he would be forced to will it; and after he had led destiny awhile by the nose, he had enough human pride and human spite to will it voluntarily.

So much is true: that the others, no matter how much they may have plotted, began their actual warlike preparations only when those of Prussia had turned to certainty the great and general mistrust. As early as the spring of this year 1756 Frederick had sent a corps to Stolp under Field-marshal Lehwald; and further, ostensibly to safeguard Hanover, he took measures to bring up the Westphalian troops and strongly provisioned the Silesian fortresses. His own officers had shaken their heads. After the middle of June, "*Alarmzustand*" was declared in East Prussia as well as Silesia, all leaves were cancelled, the reserves called in before the end of the regular manœuvres. One army was by then completely mobilized; it stood in Farther Pomerania ready to act as reserve in East Prussia. The plan of campaign, drawn up by the King together with General von Winterfeld, had long been ready, save for details. Winterfeld, a sort of general chief of staff, sat bent over route plans and lists. Everywhere horses were being bought. General von Retzov was intendant in the field. The files were formed, the marching order of the army in three great divisions was settled upon. The machine was working smoothly. And Kaunitz smiled and compressed his lips. " His Majesty of Prussia," he said, " is already making the second great mistake in state policy. First Westminster, and now these preparations. It is good we have not armed up to now, it might have spoilt everything. Now we and Russia have all the provocation in the world to hurl our troops against the boundary." And Austria set up an extraordinary armament commission; it brought its regiments on a war footing and concentrated them in Bohemia and Moravia.

On the tenth of July, Frederick ordered his generals to Potsdam; appeared among them and without more ado declared that the war must begin. " That it must," Winterfeld supported him. " Impossible! " said all the rest; and advised strongly against it. They were Prussian generals: Haudegen, Schwerin, Keith, Retzov, Schmettau, Ferdinand von Braunschweig; but they all most strenuously advised against it. The King's brother could not trust his ears. " Are we to understand," cried Prince Wilhelm, " that Your Majesty hopes to conquer this overwhelming strength? The greatest powers in Europe, the public opinion of the continent, are against us. And justice — ah, Sire, it is not on our side! " " To want to wrest victory from superior power like that is to court defeat at the hands of Providence! " So cried the princes Henry and Ferdinand. Frederick pished and pshawed, and jeered at them and said

190

they might stop at home if they were afraid. At which they naturally fired up and said that obedience was higher than personal opinions.

In the whole world he had not one moral support. England never ceased to warn him not to invoke certain destruction — against which she would be powerless to save him. But when in the middle of July he learned that Austria was mobilizing all along the line, he had the question put in Vienna, which sounded dangerously like an ultimatum: was the mobilization directed against him? Probably he had in mind to spring the combination by showing a brusque deportment. If they came to blows in midsummer, he reckoned, then Russia was not likely to march that year. Perhaps, even, English gold would keep her still, or there would be a change of thrones — for the Little Mother was not in the best of health, her love-affairs were bad for her. And France: she had signed the Treaty of Versailles, but nothing is easier than to deny the *casus foederis* if you do not want it and cannot have it. And it seemed to the King like a case of cannot.

But if France and Russia did fall away, would Austria stand up to him alone? Frederick did not think it, he did not hope for it. But if, said he, they were really with child by war, he was ready to play the midwife. A detestable figure! And another allusion to the sex of his opponent.

They were not ready yet, in Vienna. So they delayed for two weeks with their answer. Then it came. Maria Theresa explained that in the universal crisis she had taken steps to secure herself and her allies, which were not intended to

191

injure anybody. Kaunitz told her what to say — disingenuous, time-taking rubbish. Frederick still pressed. He sent word that he could not remain in ignorance of Austria's agreement with Russia. If Her Majesty could not give him, in good set terms, without employing any of the usual Austrian evasions, the assurance that she would not attack him within the next two years, then she would have her own exalted self to thank for whatever consequences might ensue upon her silence. That this demand did not admit of any discussion was obvious. Frederick's own ambassador hardly found the courage to transmit it. But simultaneously with his ultimatum Frederick in quick succession mobilized first the Pomeranias, then the Westphalias, Silesia, Brandenburg, and lastly the Berlin garrison. In six days the troops were in fighting trim and only needed a few days to reach their rendezvous. Schwerin with thirty thousand men was in Silesia. The three columns, commanded by the King in person, pushed toward a certain frontier. . . . Everything was buried in the profoundest mystery; not even the divisional commanders were informed. But there was still a delay. . . . What was Vienna's answer? After full three weeks she haughtily replied: the first steps toward mobilization had been Prussia's. Further, the alliance with Russia had existed for a decade, and was not offensive in its character — from which it followed that Prussia's anxiety was groundless. — Kaunitz again. Between the lines could be read: " If you swallow that, then you are a fool, and we shall brush you aside. If you don't, then you are a criminal disturber of the peace. Take your

192

choice." — Frederick gave the order to cross the Saxon frontier.

The Saxon frontier! Why, but Saxony was neutral, wasn't she? Saxony was not playing! — That was all one; on the twenty-ninth of August Frederick, with sixty thousand moustaches, invaded Saxony.

What a hubbub arose in Europe at this unheard-of breach of the peace, this attack on the rights of nations! We have no idea — or, rather, yes, perhaps just lately we have had an idea. But let us listen to Frederick before we listen to Europe: according to him his breach of the law was due to the following reflections and considerations. He had to be absolutely certain of Saxony, in order that she might not fight on the wrong side when she had the chance. Things must not go as they had in '44, when Saxony had stuck a dagger in his back. By occupying the country and disbanding the army or incorporating it in his own, he should have a secure base for his operations against Bohemia. As for neutrality, there was none, in any true sense of the word. In her heart, and with all her evil-disposed intentions, Saxony was with the coalition, though cowardice prevented her from admitting where she stood. Frederick, in breaking the letter of the law, in violating a neutrality that stood on paper, whereas its own betrayal did not so stand, was actuated by the sternest necessity. He had to take the guilt upon his own shoulders in order to bring it home to his enemies; he had to get hold of the archives of the state of Dresden, that nest of treachery, in order to be able to prove to all the world how Saxony had manœuvred. If Saxony were wise, she would offer no opposition; she would let him get across the mountains without delay. But let her persist in carrying her skin to market for Austria, and he would crush her once for all. When Schwerin repulsed an invasion into Silesia, and Frederick surprised them by appearing in Bohemia, then Maria Theresa might perhaps think better of it? With just one slash, perhaps, he would have cut the web that bound him, so that the severed pieces floated harmless away? Of course, the opposite result was conceivable: the various combinations still in a fluid state about him might crystallize at his touch, just as ice-cold water in a basin will begin to freeze when shaken. But one way or the other, things must be brought to a head.

Thus Frederick. But Europe had no mind at all for such balancings and experimentations. Europe shrieked as with one voice. It was terrific to hear her. The public, of course, had no " *Kujons* " in its pay; it was not posted as to preliminaries, and in its eyes the march into Saxony had taken place in the middle of the profoundest peace and was a shameless breach of international law, an attack so wanton and unprovoked that it put one quite beside oneself. To fall in force upon a neutral country, a good, innocent country which was not at all expecting such a barbarous onset and had only lately placed its army on a pathetically small peace footing, twenty-two thousand men, in order to enable Brühl to buy more wigs and coaches and scent-bottles! It was insufferable, it rent the heart, it could not and must not be that this snuff-taking Satan should tread under the heels of his top-boots all morality, all justice, all humanity, all that ennobled life, all that the upright must needs believe in. So Europe shrieked and continued to shriek; and loudest of all shrieked Austria, pointing her finger at Frederick and crying over and over again: " Now you see, don't you? There you are! "

And, as a matter of fact, Saxony was not in the least resolved on fight. She had plotted, but she was not in the least resolved. However, she was carried away by the general indignation, which confirmed her in a false and sentimental conviction of her own innocence and the justice of her cause; and she elected to perform the rôle of martyr in the cause of Austria and the rights of nations — a choice which could not save her from imminent destruction. It was impossible to withstand the masterly entry of the Prussian troops, carried out as it was with the utmost order and discipline. The defence hastily fell back on the Bohemian frontier, and let Wittenberg, Torgau, Leipsic, let Dresden, let the whole electorate fall without a blow into Frederick's hands, into the power of Prussia. The Saxon army stopped at Pirna, in a fortified position, and thither came Augustus, in flight from Dresden.

This prince, otherwise rather slack, now displayed an astonishing obstinacy, backed up by the moral support of all Europe. What Frederick demanded of him was pretty thick, after all: it was no more, and no less, than an offensive alliance against Austria, and the oath of fealty of the Saxon troops. In other words, Saxony was to link her fate, for better or worse, with Prussia's; since, as Frederick said,

Saxony and Prussia were indispensable to each other and it was to their mutual advantage to stick together. We have learned since then that mutual advantage counsels a permanent alliance not only to Prussia and Saxony, but to Prussia and Austria as well. But they had not got so far on in those days; and Frederick's theory, in the circumstances under which it was set up, must have sounded Satanic indeed. " How should I," asked Augustus in numerous letters, " turn my sword against a princess who has never given me any ground for doing so? It is my intention not to take any part in this war . . . my integrity, which I have preserved up to my sixtieth year, encourages me to reply to Your Majesty that you have possessed yourself of my territory without any justification. Europe will be the judge of my cause, and of the genuineness of the schemes you lay at my door, of the non-existence of which all the courts of Europe are convinced. . . . It seems Your Majesty can secure himself in no way save through the destruction of my army, either by the sword or by famine. Until the second happens it still lacks much; and with regard to the first, I have hopes that in the divine protection and in the constancy and loyalty of my troops I shall rest secure from the ultimate event." They were good, moving letters that poor King Augustus wrote, prompted by his consciousness that he had Europe with him. He addressed his army just as touchingly. They would, he said, thrust toward Bohemia together — which was sheerly impossible — despite the strength of the enemy. He was resolved to sacrifice his life in the attempt; it belonged to his subjects; it was for them

to save the honour of their king, and to defend him to the
last drop of their blood.

The camp at Pirna was surrounded, and the pinch was
soon felt. But until hunger enforced surrender (for Frederick wished to shed no blood, he wanted to amalgamate
the Saxon troops with his own), much precious time was
lost, time of which Austria made good use. Frederick
stopped in Dresden, where he sought by means of ingratiating forms to make his Draconian regulations more palatable; his purpose being to win over public opinion by prov-
ing from the Saxon archives the necessity he had been
under. But here too he encountered resistance so embittered
that in breaking it down he brought the world, if that were
possible, even more than ever about his ears. The state
papers were in the castle, in the custody of the Queen of
Poland, who was living there with her children. Frederick
she loathed; and she stoutly resisted all his efforts to get
hold of the documents. Frederick, however, was not the
man to shrink from using force against a lady. He sent a
general to the Queen, with definite instructions to procure
the casket in which the documents were, using force if
necessary. The scene in the Queen's apartments is variously
depicted. In any case it must have been extremely humiliating to Augustus's wife. She fought with all her strength and
with all her pride against surrendering the papers. We are
told that she defended with her own body the door to the
cabinet; other accounts say that she sat on the chest where
they were kept; others, again, that the casket was in her
bed, and that Frederick's general, after prostrating himself,

did not hesitate to violate this place too. In the end the Queen had to comply, and Frederick got the papers. He speedily had them published. But the advantage of publication was outweighed by the harm done by this fresh evidence of his brutality. The Queen called the foreign ambassadors together, gave them a vivid account of what had happened, and declared that all the rulers of Europe had been insulted in her person. Her daughter, who was dauphine in France, threw herself publicly at the feet of Louis XV and implored him, with sobs, to avenge her mother's sufferings — a scene which moved all Europe to tears of sympathy and righteous anger. The French envoy in Berlin received orders to break off relations peremptorily. The Prussian ambassador was forbidden the court at Versailles. Add to all this that the Queen of Poland died soon after, killed, so everybody said, by the ignominy she had suffered. For Frederick retorted upon her conspiracies and agitations by having her closely watched, and she was not spared further affronts. The King of Prussia, so we are told by Count Vitzthum, treated the Queen not like a person of royal blood, but like a canteen woman imprisoned in the middle of a hostile army. And it killed her. The indignation against Frederick was boundless.

It was, in fact, so deep and general that a heart less stout, a temper less sardonic than his might have quailed before it — yes, perhaps even this heart did sometimes quail. In France, a country where he had close intellectual ties, he passed for a savage, simply; they called him nothing but the barbarian, the " monster of the north." Indeed, he might have searched the whole globe over for a sign of sympathy and understanding and found none — no spot on earth where he did not pass for the enemy of mankind, a ravening beast, to draw whose fangs would be a moral act and a safe-guard to the public. He must be struck down, must be rendered for ever powerless. Not only must Silesia be taken from him; Prussia must be reduced to the position which was hers before the Thirty Years' War, the king of it once more a petty marquis, powerless for harm. Yes, the hour had struck when the civilized states must root out the Prussian spirit and rid the planet from this poisonous growth. Even those who could still think objectively had to admit that there was nothing left for Prussia but to sink under the scorn and hatred heaped upon her by the world.

Quite aside from the material resources which such hatred had at its disposition, the hatred remains in and for itself a thing to shudder at. To fear that which is of the spirit is no disgrace; it involves less cowardice than does fear of physical force. It is upon the imponderables that the best hopes of victory are based; thus there is nothing weak or foolish about taking cognizance of the imponderable and the irrational where it sides against you. The hatred and revulsion which Prussia roused might be as uninstructed and misguided as ever; but the question which had to be raised was this: was it conceivable, or humanly possible, that one man could bear up against the weight of so general a feeling and carry off the victory? It takes more constancy of spirit to confront a preponderance of moral feeling than to defy a superior body of troops.

Frederick had to admit to himself that in case of his defeat the world's rejoicing and the world's scorn would alike be unbounded; that he should get no justice, and not only that, but that he should actually have been in the wrong. Even on this ground, it was bitterly necessary for him to conquer. He was not in the right, in so far as right is a convention, the voice of the majority, the judgment of humanity. His right was the right of the rising power, a problematical, still illegitimate, untested right, which had first to be fought for and won. Defeated, he was the most wretched of adventurers — *un fou*, as Louis of France called him. Only when success had shown him to be the agent of destiny, only then would he be in the right, and proved to have been always in the right. For every deed that deserves the name is in truth a trial of fate, an effort to create a right, to guide destiny and realize the course of development. And the hatred felt against the doer of the deed is, psychologically speaking, nothing else than an effort to influence the verdict of fate against him — a naïve and irrational effort, because the verdict is settled beforehand, but still a spiritual weight and pressure which might well frighten the bravest. King Frederick is called the Great, not only because of the audacity with which he laid siege to destiny, but also and especially because he had the strength to bear up — alone, with almost superhuman nervous strength — under so heavy a burden of hate. But all the bitterness of soul, all the cynic disbelief in justice, which characterizes him who thus tempts fate, speaks in those words he uttered: "Poor mortals that we are! The world judges our acts not accord-

200

ing to our motives, but according to their success. There is nothing left for us but to achieve it."

So now they got their forces together, bodies of troops, armies, in almost ridiculous superfluity, to overcome him and carve him up in the shortest possible time at the least expense to each of them. Each one looked forward to his share. Elizabeth of Russia displayed great tenacity, she was far from dead yet, she hastened to join the Versailles concordat and signed a special understanding with Austria, by virtue of which she was to send eighty thousand men against Frederick and harry the Prussian coast with her fleet. France, which up to now had let herself be entreated, showed suddenly a hysterical zeal. By the invasion of Saxony, she shrieked, the Peace of Westphalia had been violated, shamefully violated, and the honour of all the guarantors of that peace demanded that they speedily unite to execute the evil-doer. A second Versailles Treaty arose, stating that France would contribute a hundred thousand men and pay twelve million gulden of yearly subsidy to Austria, until such time as the latter was once more secure in the possession of Silesia, and Prussia reduced to the dimensions she had before the Thirty Years' War (according to which contract France ought still to be paying to this day). The war against Prussia, the alliance with Austria, was now so popular in Paris that the French Academy offered a prize for the best verses in praise of it; but the French government found the idea silly and suppressed the offer. And that was not all. Frederick found that he had fallen foul of the " Empire." His act, they said, was a breach of peace of the "*Reich*." The Emperor commanded him to cease his unheard-of and wicked sedition, to indemnify King Augustus and withdraw from Saxony. He ordered all Frederick's generals to leave their godless lord, and not to partake in his hideous crime. And as all that did not in the slightest avail, the whole of Germany (that blind Germany!) rose against Frederick, sixty princes declared that his proceedings constituted a predatory attack, and an imperial punitive campaign was solemnly resolved upon. Sweden, one of the signatories to the Westphalian Peace, and in leading-strings to France, had perforce to resign herself to the conquest of Pomerania. And thus populations to the tune of a hundred million rose against some five; fourteen princes against one; seven hundred thousand of troops against two hundred and sixty thousand. Frederick was putting it mildly when he said he was risking his skin. Nobody had any doubt it would be all up with him in the shortest possible time.

It will give me the very greatest pleasure to cite from his letters of the period. They have a way of making one's memory act in a contrary direction — namely, forward and not back, a distinctly thrilling kind of memory.

To the Marquis d'Argens in Berlin: "The French have gone mad. You cannot imagine the disgraceful things they are saying about me. You would think that the whole salvation of France depended on the house of Austria; and the Dauphine's dreams have made much more impression than my manifesto against Saxony and the Austrians. In short, my dear friend, I deplore the consequences

202

of the earthquake that has addled the brains of all the statesmen in Europe, and I wish them peace, health, and contentment."

To Privy Counsellor von Knyphausen of the Paris legation: " It is due to the Austrian intrigues that I am obliged to recall you. When you will have left Paris, nothing will stem the tide of slander against me. My enemies will invent so many stories that the French will only see with their eyes and hear with their ears. Well, if they want to be my enemies, very well; it is their own choice."

To his sister of Bayreuth: " But since things have been pushed to this point, we must hope now that Providence, if it deigns to mix in poor human affairs, will not permit the arrogance and malice of my enemies to triumph over my just cause."

To Schwerin: " We shall have, my dear Marshal, to confront many foes — but I am not afraid. I have capital generals, admirable troops, and if heaven preserve my understanding I hope also to give a good account of myself. . . . But we must exert ourselves to the uttermost, we must crush our enemies, we must fear no numbers, but rather count it an honour that such a difficult task is ours to perform. We pay rope-dancers, but not men who merely walk on solid ground; so in this world all the glory is for those who triumph over difficulties. Farewell, my dear Marshal, I embrace you."

To his sister Amalie: " The coming campaign is to me what Pharsalus was to the Romans, or Leuctra to the Greeks, or Denain to the French, or the siege of Vienna to the Austrians. Such epochs are decisive, they change the face of Europe. Before the decision one must endure fearful hazards; but afterwards the sky is again clear and bright. Our duty is now not to despair, but to foresee each event, and bear with quiet countenance what Providence vouchsafes us, without arrogance at good fortune, or depression at bad."

To his sister of Bayreuth: "Germany is facing a severe crisis. I must defend her freedom, her privileges, and her religion. If I am defeated this time, it will be in this cause. But I am of good cheer; and however great the number of my foes, I have faith in the goodness of my cause, the admirable courage of my troops, and their steadfast will, from the commanding officer down to the lowest soldier."

To the same: "I am in the position of a traveller surrounded by a band of rascals and about to be murdered in order that the murderers may divide their booty among themselves. Since the League of Cambrai there has been no instance of a conspiracy such as this villainous triumvirate has forged against me. The thing is contemptible, a disgrace to humanity and human morals. Has the world ever seen such a spectacle as three powerful princes banding themselves together to destroy a fourth who has never done them any harm? I have never had any differences either with France or with Russia, and certainly not with Sweden. . . . *O tempora, O mores!* One might as well be living among tigers, leopards, and lynxes as in this supposedly so civilized century, contemporary of the murderers, thieves, and perjurers who govern this poor world.

Happy is he, my dear sister, who lives unknown, and has been wise enough from his youth up to abjure any kind of fame! Since no one knows him, none can envy, and his happiness cannot make him the prey of every sharper. . . . They have laid a plot against me, and the court of Vienna has been pleased to insult me; this was more than my honour could endure. So the struggle begins and the band of rascals fling themselves upon me; such is my fate."

To Minister von Finckenstein: "Be not so fearful. Nothing is lost as yet and nothing desperate. So long as I am alive I will stand firm and defend myself like a lion."

To his sister of Bayreuth: "We must all console ourselves with the thought that our century is an epoch in the history of the world, and that we have witnessed events so extraordinary that the course of things has not for long brought forth their like. That means much for our curious minds, but little for our happiness. Well, these villains of emperors, empresses, and kings are forcing me this coming year to dance upon a tight-rope. I console myself with the hope of giving one or another of them a good crack over the nose with the balance-pole. But when that is done, then peace must finally ensue. What a sacrifice of men! What horrible butchery! I shudder to think of it. But I must steel my heart and arm myself for murder and massacre; I must face the odds heroically; though they are always frightful when you see them close at hand."

To Earl Marischal Keith: "You say my enemies malign me, even in the far-away Escorial. I am used to that. I hear nothing but untruths about myself. I have had more than my fill of the vulgar lies and contemptible libels spread by hatred and venom all over Europe. But one can get used to anything. Louis XIV must get just as sick of the flatteries that are poured into his ears as I am of the shameful things they say about me. These are unworthy weapons, which a great prince ought never to employ against his peers; for he inevitably lowers himself at the same time and exposes to the scorn of the vulgar things which it is to the common interest of princes to hold in honour."

To Finckenstein: " It seems unhappily that we are not yet at the end of our task. We have too many enemies to be able to gain such superiority over them as to enforce peace. All Europe is marching against us; it seems to be the fashion to be our enemy, and a title of honour to contribute to our destruction."

To Voltaire: " You, who do not fight yourself, do not for God's sake laugh at others; be tranquil, be happy, that you have no persecutors, and learn to be care-free and enjoy the repose you have at last attained after chasing after it for sixty years. . . . Are you still, at sixty, so lacking in common sense? And learn, in your old age, how you ought to write to me. Please note that certain liberties are permitted to writers and wits; but when they become impertinent it is too much. . . . But enough, I have forgiven all, in a truly Christian spirit. On the whole, you have given me more pleasure than pain. Your writing has more power to cheer me than your scratches to hurt. . . . You cry out for peace so loudly that I am fain to tell you to turn that lofty impertinence of yours, which so well becomes you, against those who are responsible for the delay in concluding peace. . . . Despite all your efforts, I will never sign a peace save on conditions consonant with my country's honour. The people of your native land, puffed up as they are with folly and vanity, may rely upon it that I mean what I say."

To Ferdinand of Brunswick: "Unless France signs a peace with England we are hopelessly lost; we have too many enemies, too many people are disheartened by our disasters, and the morale of our troops has plainly deteriorated. There is nothing left but for you to think up an inscription for my tombstone. The great calamity will not come to pass before the middle of August; but by then all will be lost beyond repair. You know that I am usually not a pessimist; but now there is no possibility of seeing anything else but black."

To d'Argens: "The French are amusing asses. I like an enemy that makes me laugh; I hate my grumpy Austrians, swollen with impudence and pride, no good for anything except to make one yawn."

To the same: "You value life as a sybarite, I look at death like a stoic. Never will I survive that moment in which I am forced to sign a disadvantageous peace; no eloquence, no inducement, can drive me to subscribe to my own disgrace. I have told you, and I repeat: never will I put pen to a shameful peace. I am firmly resolved to stake all upon this campaign, to perform the most desperate deeds, to conquer or find an honourable end."

" The defence," says Rancke, " earned him high esteem
in the states of Europe. In defending himself, King Frederick became the great man of his century." — That is true,
and yet not true — in so far, that is, as it considers Frederick's war against Europe to have been a purely defensive
one. The dispute among historians as to whether it really
was that — and not rather a war of aggression — waxes
louder than ever today; but the situation is far too complicated, too involved, to permit of a simple and final
answer. In its very last analysis this gigantic struggle was
an offensive war; for the young, the rising power is always,
psychologically speaking, the aggressor, and the others,
the existing powers, are on the defensive against it. Somewhat more superficially speaking, it was a defensive war,
for Prussia was actually " encircled " and was to be destroyed with all possible speed. Then it was, again, an offensive war in that Frederick obligingly picked the quarrel.
Yet, once more, it was a war of defence, for when the odds
are one to five, that is tantamount to defence, even though it
was the one who actually declared war against the five —
or, rather, as a matter of fact, failed to declare it. And,
fifthly, it was an offensive war: on the ground that the
most desperate and difficult defence must always needs
save itself by attacking. " Attack, attack! Keep on their
heels! *Attaquez donc toujours!* " To that tune, instinctively,
he had always disciplined his troops, he had even made it
instinctive with them; and to it he carried on war, unmindful of the voices of those who urged him to keep on the
defensive — in situations like that of the year 1759, when

the Russians were on his left, and Daun on his right, and Sweden in his rear.

What friends he had were not worthy of the name. England regarded him as her soldier against France, she was satisfied to have him hold France in check in Europe while she quietly annexed the French colonies in the New World; but, in the interests of business, she refused to relieve him in the Baltic, against Russia; she paid subsidies as long as it pleased her, and when it pleased her no longer she left off. As we know, the war lasted seven years — seven is always the number of years the princes and the miller's sons have to serve in the fairy-tale; but it was a seven years' test a little severer than ever falls to their lot; it was, without exaggeration, the severest test ever a human soul has had to stand upon this earth. To stand it required such passive and active qualities, such a measure of endurance and patience, of inventive and resourceful energy, as neither before nor since, to my knowledge, a man has ever displayed or had occasion to display. Seven years long did King Frederick march hither and yon, fighting, beating here one enemy and there another, being beaten himself too, sometimes almost destroyed; staggering erect again because he thought of something else which might still be tried; trying it, with incredible, improbable success and coming safe off once more. Always in his shabby uniform, booted and spurred, with his uniform hat on his head, breathing, year in, year out, the dust of his own troops, in an atmosphere of sweat, leather, blood, and powder smoke, he would walk up and down in his tent, between two

209

battles, a dismal defeat and an incredible victory, and play on his flute, or scribble French verses, or write quarrelsome letters to Voltaire. His mother died, without his even seeing her; he felt now more forsaken than ever. His favourite sister died — "*mon Dieu, ma sœur de Bayreuth!*" — and his anguish at the loss testifies to the tenderness of his iniquitous heart. In time he himself became grotesque; he was not unconscious of the frightful comicality of his existence, he compared himself with Don Quixote, with the Wandering Jew. "The ox must plough the furrow," he would say, "the nightingale must sing, the dolphin swim, and I — I must make war." He imagined himself condemned to carry on war up to the day of judgment; he became a spectre to himself. The dreadful weariness of spectres he knew, their pathetic yearning for rest. "The happy dead! They are saved from all cares and troubles." He kept poison always upon him for the last emergency; but though the last emergency seemed many times to have arrived, he did not take it, for always some other plan occurred to him, and the emergency passed. Beneath the frightful punishment, the cruel vicissitudes, the ceaseless tension, "the nicest little creature in the kingdom" aged rapidly. He lost his teeth, his hair went white on one side, his back got bent, his figure leaner and leaner, he suffered from gout. And besides that, from diarrhœa. It was, in fact, the tortures of the damned he suffered. But his fame grew apace — his transgression, his breach of the rights of nations were forgotten, but his fame as of the chosen of God grew and spread like a tree and overshadowed the cen-

210

tury. It was not alone that he routed the hosts of Marshal Soubise at Rossbach — that same Marshal Soubise who stole Alsace and set fire to the Palatinate — and became a hero to all Germany, a symbol round which their torn loyalties might once more twine. His deeds, and his sufferings, won him the sympathies of the people of all nations. Yes, his defeats not less than his victories occupied near and far the hearts of men, and the grotesque, the Quixotic flavour, in his personality helped magnify him in the popular eye and elevate him to a legendary fame: his picture, with the wry mouth, the sparkling blue eyes, the three-cornered hat, the cane, the star, the shoulder-cord — it hung in cottage and hall; while he still lived he was a hero of legend. From now on he was called *der alte Fritz:* an awe-inspiring name, to anybody with a sense of awe; for it is really in the highest degree awe-inspiring to find the dæmon become a household word and given a nickname.

He had outlived the hate, the psychic resistance, of the world; and thereby had withdrawn an indispensable prop from the morale of his foes. The rest was done by his radicalism, his readiness to go all lengths, the depth of his resolution, which seemed to his opponents at once so offensive and so frightful, like a strange and savage dog — in the end they all shuddered before him. His moral advantage was that it was always, with him, a matter of life and death, and that gave him a sense of absolute values of which the others knew nothing. I will not speak of his genius as a strategist, being a layman in that field. And I wish not to speak of his " luck "; for it is always stupid to distinguish luck from a man's other merits and count it as undeserved, instead of part of all the rest. Still, if you like, he was lucky. He was on the brink of destruction when Elizabeth of Russia surrendered to her love-affairs and left a poor simpleton named Peter to reign, said Peter admiring Frederick to the point of idolatry, so that he struck a peace with him at once. But the King had to win a few more battles before the others saw at last that it was hopeless, and retired from the field tired out. He went back home.

He had won nothing tangible, and his territories were ravaged, depopulated, impoverished, run wild. But Prussia endured, not a village lost; Silesia was safe, and the end and aim of the Great Coalition a total failure. It was a deep humiliation for the continent at the hands of a single man. The verdict of destiny, all the probabilities to the contrary, had been rendered in his favour; it was impossible to dispute it in the long run. They had to make way for Prussia, for Germany, to follow its own path — a path which has since proved as steep and fateful, as full of manifold and instructive turns of fortune, as any path a people ever trod.

As for him, his later course, which continued yet for a long time, was dreary, and chilly, and unlovely. After that frightful seven years his nature had grown more sardonic than ever before. He had fought and suffered beyond the capacity of ordinary men; and to him they now all seemed like a childish breed, an undistinguishable rabble. It is incomprehensible why he should have gone on wearing himself out in labour for this breed even while he choked with scorn of it. He poured himself into the task of making good the harm that he had done, of healing the ravaged fields and patching the tattered finances, of summoning whole industries into existence, of adding a whole province to his kingdom and rescuing it from neglect by a magnificent system of colonization. And all this would be incomprehensible unless one thinks of his sense of duty as a sort of possession and of him as the tool of a higher will. His industry was a cold and joyless passion. He was burnt out, he was dry and withered and wicked, he loved nobody, and nobody loved him; his royal existence was a burden, and no honourable one, to the rest of the world. And when he needed a little animal warmth, he was fain to share his bed with his favourite greyhound. He kept a great many dogs, and it was his wish to be buried near them. When the last one of these died he wept all day long. He still found a little pleasure in embroiling his philosophers among themselves; then he sent them all away. For whereas earlier in his life he had only mocked at religion, now he mocked at philosophy as well; saying that a good digestion was more important than knowledge of the essence of things. And he had a very bad digestion, it was spoilt by the highly spiced dishes he insisted on eating. When at last he died, at seventy-four, after a tormenting and repulsive illness, everything, we are told, was deathly still, but no one mourned. There was not a single clean, whole shirt in his wardrobe, and his valet gave one of his to clothe the corpse — which was tiny as a child's.

One is prone to think of him as a sort of hobgoblin, an

object of hatred and detestation, leading the whole world into a quagmire, a spiteful, sexless troll, for the destruction of whom a hundred million men toiled to exhaustion in vain, since he was created and sent to bring about great and inevitable events upon this earth. Then, after the performance of them, he vanished, leaving behind him a husk like a little child's.

The riddle of his existence lay in the dualism which Jean Jacques Rousseau reduced to a formula: " *Il pense en philosophe et se conduit en roi.*" That is a great antithesis, and comprises many and many a pair of active opposites: for instance, right and might, thought and action, freedom and destiny, reason and dæmon, bourgeois morality and heroic necessity. Such opposites, united in one flesh and blood and become a strife of instincts, naturally do not make for a comfortable, logical, and harmonious existence. There is a resulting irony on both sides, a radical scepticism, a fanatic zeal for achievement at bottom quite nihilistic, a sense of power as melancholy as it is evil. Frederick wrote the *Antimachiavelli,* and that was not hypocrisy, but literature. He loved the humane spirit, reason, dry clarity of atmosphere — loved them by contraries and out of the depth of his being, which was essentially dæmonic, essentially a slave to the destiny which made him its instrument. Thus he loved Voltaire, the son of the spirit, the father of enlightenment and of all anti-heroic civilization. He kissed the lean hand that wrote: " I hate all heroes "; and he himself mocked his seven years' struggle with the words: " heroic weakness." But he set it down in black and

214

white that if he wanted to visit a province with the severest punishment, he would sentence it to be governed by writers; his enlightenment was so skin-deep that he believed himself bullet-proof; and when he wants to explain why he preferred the frightful strain and bloody horrors of war to the tranquil repose of a literary life, he speaks largely of a " secret instinct." What he means was stronger in him than literature; it guided his acts, conditioned his life; and it is certainly a most German thought to think that this secret instinct, this element of the dæmonic and super-personal in him, was: the urge of destiny, the spirit of history.

He was a sacrifice. He felt, indeed, that he had sacrificed himself: his youth to his father, his manhood to the State. But he erred if he believed that a choice was open to him. He was a sacrifice. He had to do wrong, he had to lead a life contrary to his thoughts, he had to be not a philosopher but a king, in order that the destiny of a great people might be fulfilled.

1914

III

AN EXPERIENCE IN THE OCCULT

AN EXPERIENCE IN THE OCCULT

Full though this world is of problems — moral, social, intellectual, artistic — weighty problems, the treatment of which must redound to the credit of any writer, shedding reflected lustre on his name and reaping him the praises of a grateful public; yet I here venture to approach you with a theme which even I myself cannot do otherwise than regard as preposterous, and, indeed, suspect. Surprise and contempt, I know, will be my portion from the general at my choice of it. But do people choose their subjects, I ask? No, they write and they talk of what they are ridden by, and nothing else; and that though the themes a man neglects may lay claim to pre-eminent importance, and the one which has taken his reason captive be actually mischievous. And all my good, respectable ideas have been vitiated by personal contacts and observations, which are at once so puerile, and yet to such a degree unexplainable (if I may talk about degrees of unexplainableness), that I cannot get away from them, and find myself, for the moment at least, spoilt for the contemplation of those more unsullied, those saner, chaster realms of thought where I could move with so much honour and credit to myself. I say spoilt. And truly it is a sort of corruption which breathes from the region I have in mind: that probably not deep, yet subterraneous region, that turbid and equivocal plane of existence, with which, in my folly, I have put myself in touch; it lures me astray from my lawful concerns to those which I know full well are none of mine, though they exercise upon my fancy and my brain a pungent attraction, like the fumes of wood-alcohol (by contrast with the bouquet from the pure wine of the spirit of civilization). Well do I comprehend how a man may fall victim to them as to a vice, and through that monomaniac, vain-foolish preoccupation be lost for ever to the moral upper world.

My case is no other than this: I have fallen into the hands of the occultists. Not precisely the spiritualists — though there were some of them too in the gathering I lately visited. But we must distinguish. The spiritualistic dogma is by no means obligatory, among the group of international scholars — not such a very small group now — whose members call themselves occultists because they are given to the study of phenomena which at present seem to us to contradict the natural order as we know it. The whole spirit-theory, as a method of explaining certain puzzles, is even, by many investigators, rejected with a gesture of stern scientific probity. And yet in fairness it must be said that in the production of occult events these scientific gentlemen do take advantage of the supra-normal, or at all events anormal disposition of certain persons who do not weigh very heavy in the intellectual scale; and that this technique (I refer, of course, to the somnambulistic state of the so-called mediums) constantly passes over into the transcendental and metaphysical. But metaphysics,

220

of course, is not spiritualism; even less is spiritualism metaphysics. The difference in degree is so great as to become a difference in kind; and it is surely quite comprehensible that philosophical metaphysics should aim to keep spiritualism at arm's length. For spiritualism — the belief in spirits, ghosts, *revenants,* spook intelligences with whom one gets into touch by interrogating a table and getting the most utter banalities by way of reply — spiritualism is in fact a kind of backstairs metaphysics, a blind credulity which is on the one hand not up to the conception of idealistic speculation, and on the other hand quite incapable of metaphysical orgies of emotion. A good example of the first alternative is Schopenhauer's masterpiece *The World as Will and Idea;* while in Wagner's *Tristan und Isolde* we possess the classic *opus metaphysicum.* And one only needs to mention these lofty flights of intuition to feel at once the lamentable triviality of the whole of that which calls itself spiritualism — though what it is is not so much metaphysics as it is a Sunday afternoon diversion for the servants' hall.

But is human dignity a criterion of truth? Yes, in a way it is. There is a man, Herr Krall of Elberfeld, well known for his famous calculating horses, a man whose trade and activities hover on the borders of the occult. I heard Herr Krall say: " If there are ghosts, then there is every reason why a man should pray for a long life; for there could not possibly be anything more insipid, childish, futile, confused, and pathetic than the existence of these creatures, to judge from their supposed manifestations." One is reminded

221

of the famous utterance of the shade of Achilles on the Cimmerian shore, the time that Odysseus held a seance there. Vain and senseless, the son of Peleus calls the existence of the dead; and, after all, the pagan world might so conceive the life after death, without making any mistake about this one as truth, fact, or dogma. On the other hand, it would go very much against the grain for a Christian to conceive another world in which things were even paltrier, stupider, and more futile than they are in this our earthly sphere; and when, as indeed it may easily happen, an intelligence knocks on a table and introduces itself to society as the spirit of Aristotle or Napoleon Bonaparte, only to belie the statement by a hundred blunders, gaucheries, and obviously intentional shufflings, then I think we are justified, on grounds of taste, in the conclusion that this is not only not Aristotle or Napoleon, it is nobody at all, but only acting as though it were; and that any complaisance toward such goings-on is beneath all human dignity.

Now, this would all be well and good if only there did not linger a doubt whether dignity and good taste are absolute criteria in the field of science, in the search for truth, in that process, in short, whereby nature explores herself through the mind of man. Dignity there is only in the province of pure spirit; and metaphysics, in the sense of transcendental speculation in the theory of knowledge, belongs to that province. But when metaphysics becomes empirical; when it condescends, or begins to feel the obligation, or yields to the temptation, to track out the riddle of the universe *experimentally* — and that is what it does in occult-

222

ism, which is nothing but empirical, experimental meta-physics — then it must not count on keeping its hands clean or its bearing stately. The only dignity it has left is the irreducible remnant that must cleave to all honourable service in the cause of truth; and it must make up its mind that it will have to deal with a great deal of filth and foolishness. For mediumism and somnambulism, the sources of occult phenomena, are a mixing of suprasensual mysteries with the mystery of organic life; and the result is turbid. There is no longer any talk of taste, of mental or spiritual *niveau*, or of the beauty of rashness. For here nature takes the field; and nature is an equivocal element: impure, obscene, spiteful, dæmonic; while man, proud man, in his very essence opposed to her, loves to put on an aristocratic air and find his own peculiar dignity in forgetting that he is a child of nature just as much as he is a child of spirit. And yet, if one were seriously, on humane grounds, to forbid mataphysics to become experimental — that is, to practise occultism — that would be to deny to natural research, to knowledge of nature in general, every human value and importance, as did the Middle Ages and the Church. As though the exact natural sciences themselves stop at the point where an encounter with metaphysics becomes unavoidable! The fact that I know and understand very little of the famous doctrines of Einstein (except that, more or less, things have a fourth dimension — namely, time) prevents me as little as it does every other intelligent layman from seeing that in this doctrine of relativity the border-line between mathematical physics and metaphysics

223

has become fluid. Is it still " physics," or what is it, when they tell us — and they are telling us today — that matter is ultimately and inmostly not material, it is just one manifestation of energy, and its smallest parts, which are neither small nor large, are, though surrounded indeed by time-spatial fields of power, themselves timeless and spaceless?

But enough of theorizing. Let us get on to my experiences. They begin at my acquaintance with a man about whom opinions have been of late strongly divided, some finding him a charlatan and traitor betrayed, others respecting him as a genuine and meritorious investigator, and one of the initiators of a new science. He is Dr. Albert Freiherr von Schrenck-Notzing. A practising physician, from a family of physicians, specialist in nervous diseases, sexual pathologist, he more than thirty years ago arrived at the study of the occult by the route of hypnotism and somnambulism. It appears that for a time he leaned toward spiritualism; but today he rejects it, and refers all the unexplainable phenomena he evokes and observes to the operation of unknown but natural forces, which will in time be recognized as such.

The appearance of his book *Phenomena of Materialization*, a few years before the war, produced a full-grown public scandal. From the official and learned world came a perfect hail of protests against such a combination of credulity, confused thinking, and fraud. The public, in so far as it came to hear about it at all, held its sides with laughter; and really the book was a severe trial of our seriousness, as to both text and illustrations — photo-

224

graphs which struck one as at once silly and grotesque. Evidence was not lacking that Dr. Schrenck-Notzing had been bamboozled — and this was probably true in more than one case. Most unfortunately, the mediumistic faculty, however genuine, is no guarantee of good character. On the contrary, it even seems to have a perfect flair for mystification. Anyhow, it looked for years as though Schrenck-Notzing had irretrievably damaged his good name as a scholar.

The years passed. The war came and with it undreamed-of chances and changes. When the second volume of *Phenomena of Materialization* came out, it was in an entirely altered atmosphere. Not that the second volume was less crazy than the first, or that the official world of science, the press, or the public welcomed it more cordially than before. No, there was no stinting of scorn and contumely. But both seemed to lack conviction, to be less fortified than before by comfortable self-assurance. There was a mild resignation, a fatalistic *laissez-faire* in the air. People had borne so much they never dreamed of bearing, such outrageous experiences had been their lot, that even their honest indignation lacked the right ring; it betrayed an unmistakable tendency to compound.

In politics there is always a right and a left wing. So in the scientific world there is, with reference to the occult, a strongly conservative and a radical-revolutionist position, together with all sorts of shadings and gradings between, on the one hand, obstinate denial of all rationally unexplainable but persistently reported manifestations like telepathy, true-dreaming, and second sight, and, on the other, a fanatical and uncritical credulity, based, this last, less on a solid reverence for the mystery than an inhuman prejudice against all reason and science. And the intransigent conservative position has a good deal on its side — as, after all, it has in politics too. For between the right and the left lies an inclined plane where it is only too easy to slip; to concede belief in one single case of the occult is to reach your little finger to a devil who almost infallibly ends by taking the whole hand and therewith the whole man. *Principiis obsta!* There is beginning to prevail in Germany today a dangerous liberalism in the camp of orthodox science — in Germany, which might hitherto have been regarded as the stronghold of conservatism in this respect. Abroad — in England, in France — there had always been a more yielding temper, and more often displayed. (I will not speak of America, where an unnecessary amount of humbug seems to have got mixed up with occult studies.) Perhaps we Germans were influenced by the fact that Schrenck-Notzing's book was translated into English; that the Society for Psychical Research two years ago summoned to London his principal medium, a person named Eva C., and published a very serious report of the sittings with her; that French savants like Richet, Flammarion, Gustave Geley, Dr. Bourbon, and others supported this report in its boldness, tested its experiments, confirmed its results. All in all, a slight shakiness is evident, a certain demoralization of our conservative and sceptical front. There are traitors, and the traitors are secret before they

226

become public. There are university professors, and not only philosophers and psychologists, but natural scientists, physicists, physiologists, and physicians, who take advantage of the bad street-lighting in Munich to steal like conspirators to the evening sittings of Herr von Schrenck-Notzing to see what it does not profit them to see. For they must know, and they do, that the only way of remaining intact is to shut their eyes and not see. They are lost, or as good as lost, it is all up with their scepticism — or, rather, their scepticism *begins* — when they see. There are instances. A much-sought-after Munich oculist openly confessed that after what he had seen at Schrenck-Notzing's he had grown "very cautious in his scepticism." A charming phrase — the most equivocal phrases are usually the charmingest. For I aver that that can be no true scepticism which is not sceptical of itself; and a sceptic, in my humble view, is not merely one who believes the prescribed things and averts his eyes from everything that might imperil his virtue. Rather your true sceptic will, in ordinary language, find all sorts of things possible, and he will not, for the sake of convention, deny the evidence of his sound senses.

As for me, I have always stood, theoretically, rather far left in this business of the occult; holding, in the sense of the thoroughgoing scepticism I just defined, that all sorts of things are quite possible; but not boasting any personal or practical experience in suprasensual realms. I have rested in a theoretical benevolence. I have felt, and may have even casually expressed, a desire to attend a sitting, but nothing came of it, and that nothing came of it was probably my own doing.

And now? At the present moment? Just lately? You must let me tell the tale as it fell out. I had a visitor, an artist man from a comic paper, with an order to make a caricature of me. Very good. He drew me a crooked nose, and one thing led up to another. God knows how we came to speak of Herr von Schrenck-Notzing. Had I heard that he was working with a new medium, my guest asked, as he went on cracking jokes with his pencil. It was a youth, hardly a man yet, named Willy S., a dentist by profession and a devil of a fellow in the psychical line. Schrenck got perfectly crazy manifestations through him. He had discovered him, brought him to Munich, found him lodgings and a job, besides paying a deposit to ensure Willy's exclusive services. He had been working with him a year now, and had him so well trained, psychically speaking, that Willy, unlike most mediums, could endure an almost constant change of audience, with the rarest disappointments. That was important for Schrenck-Notzing for the sake of the propaganda. — " Might one get to see a sitting? " I asked. The artist man thought it quite possible. He knew Schrenck-Notzing, and he would like to go to one himself. Leave it to him, he would arrange an invitation.

So it came about. There followed an appointment by telephone; and one winter evening at eight o'clock, toward Christmas-time, I found myself on the tram with my caricaturist, bound for the seance. Both of us were in high spirits, exhilarated, curious, in a mood between bluster and

228

funk, something like the feelings of a young man going for the first time to a girl.

The palatial residence of Baron von Schrenck-Notzing is near the Karolinenplatz, in an exclusive quarter. We arrived, and a servant led us through a marble vestibule and up some steps to an antechamber. As we took off our things we were greeted by our host, with cool, aristocratic politeness, and ushered into a good-sized library, where the other participants in the coming seance were already gathered. Only one of them was known to me. I addressed him, expressing my surprise at finding him here. This was Professor G., the zoologist, an enthusiastic sportsman, ski-runner, yachtsman, and Alpinist, a beardless, young-looking man, though certainly in the middle forties; distinctly out-of-doorish and nature-loving — I should never have taxed him with any hankerings after the occult. Introductions followed. I was delighted to meet Emanuel Reicher, celebrated actor and hyphenated American, just then living in Germany. Then there was the medium's housekeeper and foster-mother, a widow in middle life, named Frau P. Likewise a Polish artist, blond and clean-shaven, full of friendly talk in a gruff, hearty voice. Then this and that member of the Schwabing intelligentsia. But the intellectual laity were outnumbered, on this occasion at least, by the medical men and natural scientists. There was another professor of zoology, a typical *Gelehrter*, mild and shy; a young doctor from Switzerland; a still youthful German physician, assistant at a Munich hospital, who had brought along an apparatus to measure blood-pressure; a jolly, fair-haired lady specialist in nerve massage. . . . Many of those present were novices, Reicher for one. He seemed to have no affiliations with the occult, but merely with the social circle represented.

The medium, Willy S., kept rather in the background. The Baron introduced me to him among others. " Here," he said, " is our star performer." He repeated the phrase more than once, obviously with the idea of stimulating the young man's sense of importance, but also by way of pre-possessing me in favour of this precious and delicately organic instrument of his experiments. In my case, his concern was quite unnecessary. My sympathies were bound-less, and I took pains to let our artist feel that I was no hostile onlooker, present with the sole idea of pouncing and unmasking, with a bellow of triumph. I was a sceptic on the positive side, who would rejoice at his success — I wished him to know that. Deception? Between decep-tion and reality there were many degrees, and at some point they were one. Perhaps there was a sort of natural decep-tion, which might be just as good to talk to as reality! I had come hither, not humbugging myself in the least, to see what there was to be seen, just that, no more and no less. I exchanged a few words with Willy S. and tried to get an idea of his personality. I found a dark-haired youth of some eighteen or nineteen, not unattractive, certainly with nothing striking about him. His origins were plainly simple; his speech a South-German-Austrian dialect, and his manner decent and friendly, with no signs of wanting to curry favour by over-politeness. His answers to my mat-

230

ter-of-fact questions were monosyllabic; and he seemed, quite excusably, in a sort of stage-fright, a state of suppressed excitement united with the shyness natural to his youth.

The young clinician summoned Master Willy to have his blood-pressure measured, and I turned away and followed our host's invitation to have a look round in the laboratory adjoining. It was a large room, filled with a confusion of photographic apparatus and arrangements for a magnesium flash-light. There were tables and chairs upon which stood or lay a variety of objects: a music-box, a little table-bell with a handle, a typewriter, several white felt rings, and so on — objects uninteresting in themselves, which yet would be employed by young Willy to accomplish strange matters. We shall come back to them. There was a sort of cage made of fine wire in which they had confined the youth during a severely scientific and critical sitting. It had not prevented him from doing what they could not explain. Lastly there was the so-called " black cabinet," about which so much had been said and so much more whispered. Some of Willy's predecessors had been sorely in need of it. I looked within. There was nothing special about it. Indifferent lumber stood behind the ceiling-high curtain which shut off one corner of the room from the rest. " We shall not require the cabinet," said Dr. von Schrenck-Notzing. Willy did not need it. He was strong. He sat right out in the room in his operations. So much the better. My positive scepticism had swallowed the cabinet too — but if Willy was strong, why, so much the better. We returned

231

to the library. Beyond it lay a study with a writing-table, where Willy made his toilet for the sitting.

He did not make it by himself. By no means. He made it under the argus-eyed control of three persons: the master of the house and two assistants. This time Dr. von Schrenck appointed as assistants the lively nerve-specialist and myself. And we obliged him — though privately I doubted my fitness for the office. I felt lax and benevolent, and inclined to regard the supervision as a formality. I am not at home in the rôle of misdoubting observer; it embarrasses me, it is repugnant to my humanity. You cannot expect a man to turn you his good side when you take his bad one for granted. This youth now girding up his loins to perform marvels — why should I dash his spirits by showing him I suspected him of preparing to take me in? I am a sceptic, but I want something to happen. Yet might not that be the most fundamental and extreme form of scepticism? Perhaps I, in my laxity and benevolence, was the most unbelieving of all? — But no more, for the moment. Make your toilet, young man, I will watch you.

The Baron showed us the black, one-piece tricot affair in which Willy was to cover himself from neck to ankle. He urged us to subject it to a careful scrutiny, to feel it all over. He laid great stress on a critical attitude. A garment, of cotton tricot. Very good. No sign of deception about that; and Willy drew it on over his tanned, boyish body. As he did so I caught a shy and solemn look he cast at my colleague, the blonde lady nerve-specialist, who blithely regarded the ceiling. But in nothing but the tricot

232

the chap would freeze, that was humanly plain; so they gave him a dressing-gown besides, a comfortable old wadded kimono of the Baron's, which likewise we conscientiously examined, pockets, lining, and all. A good-natured old dressing-gown. Good. But it had one curious feature: the Baron explained it to us. It was trimmed all over with ribbons, on the sleeves, the seams, the hem, sewed on everywhere. And these ribbons had been treated with a luminous preparation so that you would be able to see the outline of Willy's figure even by a dim light and easily keep it in your eye. That seemed a sensible precaution. More luminous ribbon went like a diadem about his head; he stuck his feet into an old pair of Turkish slippers. They completed the preparations. Or no. For when he stood arrayed he opened his jaws very wide, like a lion, as though to swallow us. I gasped; until it was explained to me that this was a matter of controlling the mouth cavity. The deuce! And I had been within an ace of forgetting the mouth cavity. He already had one gold tooth in it, to the honour of his trade. For the rest, it was an irreproachable mouth cavity. We saw it as far down as the glottis. In God's name, enough. We returned to the other room.

A chorus of friendly shouts welcomed us. The old hands hailed their Willy in his professional disguise. It was a merry masquerade, and Willy himself, in his talar and priestly bands, laughed too, in good-natured embarrassment. *Allons, mes enfants!* The company trooped into the laboratory and our host shut the door behind us.

Things were looking serious. Unnatural events were to

take place in this strange room that was like a photographic studio even down to the objects to distract the children's minds with. I confess to a little faint-heartedness, an inner resistance, a doubt whether I, personally, was a suitable candidate for the enterprise. But now the conductor of the experiment, all unsolicited, entrusted me with the control of the medium, Willy's landlady, Frau P., acting as the second control; and began at once to instruct me in the technique. And technique it was, in all seriousness, very thorough and gratifying indeed. I sat opposite to the young man, with my chair close to his, his two knees between mine. I held both his hands and my assistant both his wrists. Nobody could deny — and I was far from doing so — that Willy was in safe arrest; we sat and looked idiotically at each other, while the rest of the company took their places chattering.

We were grouped in front of the curtain, in an irregular circle, three-quarters closed. At one end sat the medium, with us " controls," and at the other the master of the house. Not all those present found a place in this circle; two or three people had to move back into a second row, where they stood or sat as they liked. Among them was the sporting zoology professor, who to my astonishment had armed himself with an accordion. It appeared that he was a skilled performer on this instrument, in demand for excursions and summer evening garden-parties, and particularly welcome in such gatherings as the present one, for a medium needs music, almost continuous music, for his demonstrations — a temperamental requirement which it

234

would be foolish not to gratify. Professor G. with his concertina added variety to a programme which would otherwise have been furnished only by a music-box that played one single and not even very pleasing tune.

The room was still lighted by ordinary white electricity, by which the Baron put the finishing touches to his arrangements. A little table stood in our circle, not precisely in the middle, rather nearer to our host than to the medium, from whom it was some five feet distant. The Baron measured the distance with a yardstick, and then placed several objects upon it: a lamp in a red shade, the table-bell, a plate of flour, a little slate and piece of chalk. A sizable waste-paper-basket stood upside-down by the table, with a music-box on it; not the one that was to play (that stood on a shelf behind the Baron's chair), but a smaller affair on which Herr Willy's powers were to be displayed. The typewriter the Baron set somewhere on the carpet near himself; then he strewed felt rings about the floor within the circle. They were luminous, like the ribbons on Willy's clothes, and to one or two of them was attached a longish, luminous string. Furthermore, all the larger objects, so far as was practicable, the waste-paper-basket, the music-box, the table-bell, were marked with luminous ribbons as well. These ribbons were the Baron's own invention, he rather prided himself on them and used them in profusion. . . . The light went out.

But it was turned on again; for Willy, sitting there in my arrest and still in his waking senses, had remembered something. " The pins, Herr Baron," he said. He referred, did this honourable youth, to another precautionary measure which had been overlooked. The Baron bestuck the sleeves and skirt of the velvet dressing-gown with pins that had thick, white, illuminated heads. Others of the same kind already stuck in the curtains, right and left of the opening, so that every movement in their folds must betray itself. Once more the white light was turned off. The only illumination now was a dark red shimmer from the shrouded ceiling light, and from the little lamp on the table, which was likewise shaded. For the unadjusted eye rather a scanty illumination. But the Baron assured us that it was the best he could do. His utmost efforts had not succeeded in securing a greater toleration for light. " I struggle," he said, " for every ray, but this is all I can get, up to now." However, Willy himself gave out light; so did the felt rings, the bands on the other objects, and the pins in the curtains. After all, the field of operations was visible; and after a little while the top of the table seemed really quite well lighted. We were asked for a little silence, in which the music-box performed its single number, a clear and childish tune with a brief recurring melody and a tinkling accompaniment. We waited. I in particular waited, with Willy's hands in mine, neither too tight nor too loose.

Suddenly, after two or three minutes, he shivered. A shudder ran through him, and his arms, taking mine along, began to perform pumping and thrusting motions. His breath came short and thick.

" Trance," announced my experienced assistant.

So the chap had fallen into a trance under my hands!
236

I had never observed this state before, and gave it my profoundest attention, convinced as I am that it is a condition of the most far-reaching implications. While it lasts, Willy's ego is divided into two symbolic persons, for the purposes of his dream-performance, a male and a female. He calls them Erwin and Minna. Childishness. Hocus-pocus. Nobody takes Erwin and Minna seriously; but for the sake of the business in hand we are fain to humour the whim: from now on we ignore Willy's existence and stick to these two, who have a simple way of making clear which is which. Erwin is a lout. He manifests himself by the vigour with which Willy lays about him, but seldom does anything worth seeing; leaving the serious business to his milder and more efficient sister. My assistant thought it was Minna who was now shaking us and pumping with our arms.

" Is Minna there? " asked the Baron.

Yes, she was there. I receive one quick, firm pressure of Willy's hand; that is Minna's way of saying yes. For no there is a sideways motion of the hands and torso, to and fro. Moreover, the somnambulist will speak to the controls; his voice is a quick, loud, thick-tongued whisper, with a certain intensity in it.

The Baron greets Minna. " Good-evening, Minna. There are good friends here, most of them you know, a few are new, but you don't mind that, do you? "

A to-and-fro movement in denial.

" Today the control is a very sympathetic man, full of the most cordial interest in you and your powers. I hope you will show him something nice."

A squeeze of my hand, a short forward thrust of Willy's torso. Yes, she promises — absurdly enough, one involuntarily says " she."

"Well then, Minna, do your best."

And a general conversation begins. It has to begin, the medium exacts it. " Talk," he babbles in my ear, and I pass the word on. The company have formed a chain and are sitting hand in hand. This may be a vestige of spiritualistic parlour games, it may be an organic necessity. Hard to tell. Anyway, Willy insists on it, and keeps whispering us to keep the chain firm. My neighbour on the left is in touch with me too, his right hand rests on my shoulder and arm. We talk into the darkness, saying anything that comes into our heads, scarcely knowing to whom. It is not easy. The subject-matter dwindles, the forced conversation keeps breaking off or dying away, for our real attention is not upon it. But we are warned against watching too eagerly for phenomena. Our leader recommends a hovering attitude, a mood of suspension, which may be evoked by the music that now mingles with our loud, artificial voices. The zoology professor has struck up behind us on his concertina, wheezing out a brisk succession of lively marches. His resources are apparently endless; and when he falters, the music-box takes up the strain with its tinkling little tune.

A fantastic setting. It is not hard to see why science, which sets store by exact values, is at home in the dry, objective air of the laboratory and used to purely abstract work with apparatus and prepared subjects, should feel

238

put off with this all too human kind of experimentation. It is the same with the layman. He has come keyed up to a suggestive atmosphere and a mood of consecration and mystery. He is disappointed to find himself in a situation which probably disgusts him both intellectually and æsthetically, suggesting as it does the mawkish revival methods of the Salvation Army. This impression is strengthened by the shouts with which the audience keeps encouraging the medium — or, rather, the officiating Minna: " Hullo, Minna, are you there? Buck up, show us what you can do! Get on with it, Minna! " The one mystical thing about the situation — and that not in any spiritual sense, but with reference to organic mysteries, primitive and affecting at once — is the medium himself, as he tosses and threshes with his arms, whispering in quick groans and pants: he is the primary object of my curiosity. His condition and actions quite strikingly and unmistakably remind me of the act of parturition. The head is now thrown far back, now it sinks on my shoulder or on our hands, which are so wet with perspiration that I constantly need to renew my grip. His efforts come at intervals, like throes; the pauses between are times of complete rest and inaccessibility, during which he sleeps, the head drooping sideways on the chest, and assembles new powers. This is deep trance, from which he rouses himself to resume his procreative labour.

A masculine lying-in, in a reddish darkness, amid chatter and shoutings and jazz. It was like nothing else in the world. I reflected that it would have been quite worth seeing even

239

if nothing else were to happen. And really it looked as though nothing else would. The " child " did not come. Nothing supernatural felt inclined to show itself. True, some of our audience, in their eagerness to see things, anticipated them. Two of the illuminated pins had come out of Willy's dressing-gown, though they had been stuck in deep and firmly. They lay on the floor, one of them rather far off him. The eager said they had been taken; but it was quite possible if not probable that Willy's writhings had forced them out. But then, what about the two lighted rings which had lain immediately in front of the curtain? They had originally been visible in all their circumference, not partly hidden by the hangings; but in the course of the last few minutes their position had changed, you could see only about a third of them now; either the curtain had moved forward or the rings back, while the next time you looked, see, they were once more entirely visible, free of the curtain and not beneath it. And that was a manifestation. A poor, uncertain one, but it had to suffice. And had I not felt the breath of cooler air the medium exhaled — that always heralded new phenomena? No, to be frank, I should have welcomed any breath of cooler air, but I had noticed nothing of the sort.

And time passes. It is hard to judge how much has passed already; perhaps three-quarters of an hour. Evidently the medium is having a hard time. They ask if this is the case, but he denies it and goes on struggling. They ask if everything is in order, and the answer is yes. But I don't believe him. Privately I take on myself the blame for our lack of success. From the first I had doubted whether my nature would be helpful to the good Willy at his work; and now I am certain that there in his beyond he shares my doubts. He denies it, of course; that is the merest politeness — however odd it may sound to speak of somnambulistic politeness. So far as I can observe, it is by no means impossible that civilized and personal considerations have a hampering effect in this condition; nor did Willy absolutely deny that this was so. He said in a whisper: " Do you want the phenomena to come faster? " Well? And what then? Silence. Did he want a pause? Still silence. Then he began to kick with his feet; the Baron counted. Fifteen times. A fifteen-minute pause, then. Good. We stop, temporarily.

The medium is given time to come to before the light is turned on. He made wonderful preparations: scraping motions of hand and arm at his side, which, in his fancy at least, served to draw in the organic forces which had been sent out but not yet manifested. He woke in a series of starts and blinked stupidly at the light. We betook ourselves into the next room.

Cigarettes were lighted. Willy smoked too, sitting on the sofa in his costume. The position was discussed. It was far from being discouraging. A temporary hitch. The need of rest was not unusual. An absolutely negative sitting occurred very seldom with our Willy. Nothing was lost. Willy's foster-mother diverted us with tales of their domestic experiences. They would probably have to move into another apartment. People objected to the uncalled-for things that were always happening, wherever Willy was:

241

spontaneous phenomena, signs and wonders. Fists knocked on the walls. Hands did things nobody told them to. A spook had showed itself most unexpectedly at the dining-room door. The cook had seen it, and fled with a shriek. All that was to the good. However, as for us we had so far drawn a blank. The young clinician took a new measurement with his blood-pressure apparatus, for purposes of comparison, and discussed its result with Dr. von Schrenck. Fifteen minutes. The Baron signed for the renewal of the sitting.

I felt sure that Willy had contrived the pause in order to get the control changed, and so I insisted on giving up my office. But our host would not hear to it. No, no. We must not give way to all Minna's little whims. For the sake of the impression I should get, it was necessary I should have the medium in my personal charge. But I might take the second place, Frau P.'s, and give the first to someone else, either Herr Reicher or Herr von K. Better Herr von K. "Come on, Herr von K. You always manage to get it out of her."

Von K. was the Polish painter, the man with the gruff and hearty voice. He was a direct and vigorous character and the medium's favourite control. When a session seemed likely to be a failure, they always called on him. He held Willy's hands and encouraged him with a geniality of which he alone possessed the secret; and almost always something happened. " *Grüss' Gott, Minna!* Old friends together again, that's fine, I think, and surely you think the same? You do, eh? Right-oh — but listen to me, not so hard! You'll pull my shoulder out. Minna, is that the way

242

you love me? " Like that. Willy requires this sort of thing, and almost always responds to it. Soon after the red light went on again, he had fallen into the magnetic trance. The music-box rippled, the concertina took its turn. The lying-in went on.

My position was awkward, bent over as I was, without anything to lean on; but I clutched Willy's wrists oblivious of all else, and was shaken by his wrestling. He pulls us to and fro, he pumps and trembles, tosses and writhes, whispers with foaming lips: " Talk, talk! " " The chain, the chain! " " The chain," repeats the devoted von K. " Surely my Minna may ask that the circle be properly closed! " The longer we sit, the harder we have to try to keep the dwindling conversation going. The Baron encourages us. " Talk, gentlemen. Professor G., you are going to sleep. Herr Mann, are you talking? " " Yes, Baron, I am talking as hard as I can." The audience pulls itself together and utters the sheerest twaddle into the dark. Reicher, the actor, helps himself out with a sonorous " *Rhabarber, Rhabarber!* " The music is painful. We are weary to tears of the music-box's one tinkling little tune, but when the concertina sets in, with wheezing and puffing, then we want the harmless tinkling back again. If it is hard for Willy, it is not easy for us. Almost another hour has passed since the intermission. My back aches, but I ignore it. The medium starts out of deep trance. He gives a violent jerk, and seems to be trying to expel something by means of lurches and lunges. " Brava, Minna," von K. cajoles her. " You're on the way, we can all see that. You've only to take

243

hold, it will be wonderful, I'll like you twice as much." In vain. Not a sign. Even Herr von K.'s blandishments are without result. Resignation glides into all our hearts. For my part, I feel I have no luck with the mysteries. I shall go on as before, granting the possibility of all sorts of things; but I shall have seen nothing. Well, so much the worse for me. Dyed-in-the-wool materialists have spent evenings here. So have open enemies, protesting that the whole thing was a trick. So have irascible physicists with their insistence on the laws of nature. And one and all have come and seen and gone away with their so-called scepticism shaken. Whereas my scepticism, which by comparison with theirs is belief, a faith in nothing and everything — what name shall I give it? — will have proved essentially unproductive, nihilistic. A slight, unmistakable bitterness comes over me. Well, anyhow, the impressions of the evening have been worth taking away.

Our host tries a last expedient. He takes a high tone, and speaks: " Now, Minna, let's be fair. We have been sitting here over two hours, you cannot say we have been impatient. But everything has its limits. We'll give you another five or ten minutes, and then if nothing happens we will call a halt, and these gentlemen will go home and some of them will certainly think that you can do nothing. They will have no faith in your powers and they will say so, and the sceptics will be pleased." — " No, no," says von K., and seconds the Baron while seeming to contradict him. " No, Herr Baron, don't talk like that — isn't she just on the point of doing it? She knows best what she is about, does my Minna; she puts out her little arm, and when she has stretched it far enough — eh, what did you say? Want the music stopped? What did you say, Minna darling? "

The medium has interrupted him in a whisper. The music is still, we are all still. There comes again, in a painful stammer: " The handkerchief! "

" The handkerchief," repeats Herr von K. authoritatively. " She knows just what she is about; she is going to do it for us, is my little Minna! "

" By all means," says the Baron. " If that's all, here is the handkerchief." He takes a large fresh one out of his pocket, holds it by one corner, and drops it on the floor near the table, where it lies, a white gleam in the twilight. We all lean over and stare at it.

" Push the table further back," Willy whispers. His face is lying on his hands. Is that right? " No, not that way." He cannot see, but in his dream he knows what is going on, and that something is not as he would have it. Impatiently, just as though he saw, he tells the Baron what to do. He wants the table further over, first somewhat to the left and then nearer to our host. There. That is right. There is now more space between the table and the handkerchief. " The circle," whispers Willy; we squeeze each other's hands. " Talk," he whispers, and we hasten to comply. I begin to utter some nonsense to my neighbour the Pole, I have turned my head and begun to speak, when I hear somebody say, with artificial calm: " It's coming." I jerk my head round.

You know the place in *Lohengrin*, in the first act, after Else's prayer, when the chorus begins in unison: " *Seht!*

Welch seltsam Wunder! " It was just like that. The handkerchief had got up. It rose from the floor. Before all our
eyes, with a swift, assured, vital, almost beautiful movement it rose out of the shadow into the rays of light, which
coloured it reddish; I say rose, but rose is not the word. It
was not that it was wafted up, empty and fluttering. Rather
it was taken and lifted, there was an active agency in it,
like a hand, you could see the outline of the knuckles, from
which it hung down in folds; it was manipulated from the
inside, by some living thing, compressed, shaken, made to
change its shape, in the two or three seconds during which
it was held up in the lamplight. Then, moving with the
same quiet assurance it returned to the floor.

It was not possible — but it happened. May lightning
strike me if I lie. Before my uncorrupted eyes, which would
have been just as ready to see nothing, in case nothing had
been there, it happened. Indeed, it presently happened
again. Scarcely had the handkerchief reached the floor
when it came back up again into the light, this time faster
than before; plainly and unmistakably we saw something
clutching it from within, the members of something that
held it — it looked to be narrower than a human hand,
more like a claw. Down, and up again, for the third time
up. The handkerchief was violently shaken by the something inside it, and tossed toward the table, with a poor
aim, for it hung by one corner and then fell to the floor.

Loud shouts of applause and vivas for Minna. Several
times the Baron leaned over to ask me if I saw, if I could
see everything quite clearly. I certainly did; how could

I have helped it, unless I had shut my eyes? And I had never kept them wider open in my life. I had seen greater things on this earth, more beautiful, more worthy of admiration. But never before had I seen the impossible happening despite its own impossibility; and so I kept saying in rather a shaken voice: " Very good, very good! " though for my own part I felt anything but good. Here I sat, holding in my very own hands Willy's wrists in their tricot sleeves; while immediately next to me I saw his knees in the custody of the Pole. Not a thought, not a notion, not the shadow of a possibility that the boy sleeping here could have done what was happening there. And who else? Nobody. And still it was done. It gave me a queasy feeling.

The lifting of the handkerchief, I heard said round me, was regularly the introductory phenomenon. The spell was broken. The medium, who had been strangely still during these events, sat up with a shiver and whispered: " Put away the music-box. The bell." " The bell," cries von K., all enthusiasm. " Where is my Minna's bell? The bell, on the basket! Good, now we're off again! " The Baron obeys. He takes away the music-box and puts the bell on the waste-paper-basket, its ribbons gleaming in the dusk, and the metal shining redly. Willy carries his hands and ours to his brow. He sighs. Then the bell is taken — impossible, of course, but it is taken — by a hand, for what else can take a bell by the handle? Taken, lifted up, held high and slanting, rung violently, carried in a curve through the air, rung again, and then with a swing and a clatter flung under the chair of one of the audience.

247

Slight seasickness. Profound wonderment, with a tinge, not of horror, but of disgust. Minna's praises resound, loud and unceasingly. " Unbelievable! " one of the novices cries out. Her head — what am I saying? I mean his head, Willy's head — leans toward mine, like a little child he lays his temple against mine. Good lad, nice lad! You have done marvels. Shaken and respectful, I let his head rest against mine. But the Baron says:

" Here, Minna, is something new for you. You haven't seen it yet, but it is quite easy to use. It is a bell. You press it, strike on it from above, you see. Like this. Then it rings. You do it, Minna. Here is the bell."

And he sets it on the basket. Tense expectation. At once we hear a feeling round the bell, as though fingers were touching it uncertainly. They take it up, shake it slightly; it rings, but not in the right way.

" Not like that," says the Baron. " You don't understand. Let me show you. There, that's how it's done." He strikes the button. " The circle," whispers Willy, quivering, against my cheek. But the Baron cannot make the circle and strike the bell both at the same time. He asks Minna to realize this. Hardly has he resumed his seat when the fingering and touching begin again. At last the trick is successful. The fingers strike the bell from above, weakly, like a child; but the task is definitely performed. The clapper sounds.

" Brava, Minna," shouts the audience. " Fantastic! " somebody says. But we have no time to surrender to our sensations; for more follows. Hardly has the Baron taken away the bell, when the basket begins to move. Something knocks it, it totters and tips over; then it is lifted from the floor and held high in the air. It hangs there askew and unsteady in the red light, outlined by its illuminated ribbons, for three or four seconds long, then tumbles to the floor.

"Did you see that? Did you see that?" asks the Baron, pridefully. We admit that we are impressed. Willy hangs sideways from his chair, in deep trance. Certainly a man must stand in need of profound and dreamless sleep, after so intense a dream that the events of it are actually projected outside of him! Wait. Let me think. Let me withdraw within myself and try to divine where may be the point, when the magical moment, in which a dream-picture objectivates itself and becomes a spatial reality, before the eyes of other people. Nausea. Clearly this point does not lie within the plane of our consciousness, or of the laws of knowledge as we know them. If anywhere, it is located in that state in which I see this lad now before me, and which is certainly a gate — whither? Behind the house, behind the world? . . . But I admit that this is not thinking at all — only a mild form of seasickness.

To set things going again, the Baron starts up the music-box. He also makes a change in the control. Von K. and I are released. I grope my way in the dark to the other end of the chain and find a seat beside Reicher, who sits next my host. I have the little table before me. And scarcely have I taken my chair, and my neighbours' hands, when a fingering begins at the music-box on the table. The Baron hastens to stop the music. And in the stillness, before my eyes, that see nothing whatever, there is a scratching, rustling, and mysterious feeling-about over the handle of the instrument, a trying to turn it. Ah, you deep and immemorially light-shy creature, compact of dream and matter, what are you doing there in front of our noses? Crick, the handle is turned, the works go round. " Tell it to stop," says the Baron. At my command it stops. " Go on," I say. And the music plays. This happens several times. You sit there, bending forward, you command the impossible, and you are obeyed, by a spook, a panic-striken little monster from behind the world. . . .

A pause. Then arises a varied activity among the light rings on the floor. They are shoved to and fro, tossed from place to place. One rises from the floor with its gleaming string hanging down. It is held up, carried through space, brought to the table, where it wants to be put down, and is, with a clumsiness which might lead one to think that its motive force was blind. But probably the thing is timid, afraid of being seen, afraid of venturing too far into the circle of lamplight on the table. The ring is moved to the nearest corner of the table, by a kind of stealthy shove that makes the felt scrape along the wood. It just balances. At the same time the thing, in its blind, clumsy trepidation, knocks so hard against the table that it shakes. Tut, tut, you hole-and-corner fish out of water, why, and with what monstrous knuckles, are you knocking like that on our good table, before our face and eyes? Just as I am thinking this, plop, a ring flies into my face. Something has flung it at me, it drops on my knee and thence at my feet.

250

What a playful monster! We all laugh. But it is not amuse-ment we feel, rather a sort of sinking sensation at the chill-ing arrogance of this something or other which is perhaps only a distressingly complicated kind of humbug. But, as I said, a civilized. It did not throw the music-box in my face, but tactfully chose one of the soft little rings. People have had their ears boxed, and other practical jokes have been played, such as unlacing boots. Somebody had his wrist-watch taken off and carried about the room. But nobody, it is unanimously affirmed, has ever suffered any serious harm from these powers, and that is an indication of good sense and decent feeling. On the other hand, they do un-mistakably tend to become demoralized, to play silly tricks and make unmotivated displays of strength. The need of constant oversight, guidance, and direction is plain — as, for instance, when the agency now set to work, with a good deal of persistence, to upset the music-box standing on the table. The Baron was alarmed for his instrument, and begged Minna to spare him the heart-breaking annoyance which any kind of repair work costs in these days. In vain. " It " obstinately persisted in overturning the box, on which lay the slate and slate-pencil, likewise in danger of breaking.

Something had to be done by way of distraction, and the Baron thought of the typewriting-machine, which stood on the floor in front of the curtain, with paper inserted ready for use. " Write, Minna," he said. " Do something useful. We will listen to you, and then we shall have the writing, to prove that we are not hypnotized, as some of your enemies say." The thing seems able to listen to reason, it desists from its efforts at the box. We wait. And, on my honour, the writing-machine begins to click, there on the floor. This is insane. Even after all we have already seen, it is in the highest degree startling, bewildering, ridiculous; the fantasticality of the thing is even fascinating. Who is it writing on the machine? Nobody. Nobody is lying there on the carpet in the dark and playing on the machine, but it is being played on. Willy's arms and legs are held fast. Even if he could get an arm free, he could not reach the machine with it; and as for his feet, even if they could reach that far they could not touch single types on the machine, they would tread on several at once. No, it is not Willy. But there is nobody else. What else can we do but shake our heads and laugh? The writing is being done with the right touch, a hand is certainly touching the keys — but is it really only one hand? No, if you ask me, there are surely two hands; the sounds are too quick for one, they sound as though proceeding from the fingers of a practised typist; we come to the end of a line, the bell rings, we hear the carriage being drawn back, the new line begins — the sound breaks off and a pause ensues.

Then somewhat further back, in front of the dark background of the curtain, suddenly, swiftly, and fleetingly, the following little apparition. Something appears, a longish something, vague, and whitely shimmering; in size and general shape like a human forearm, with closed fist — but not certainly recognizable as such. It comes and goes, showing itself before our eyes, lighted by a sort of flash of white lightning that issues from its own right side and wholly obscures whatever shape it has — then it is gone.

" There, there is a materialization for you," says our host, pointing to it. " I'm glad you have seen one. Wait, perhaps it will make an impression for us." And he pleads with Minna to put her hand into the plate of flour on the table. But I did not for a minute believe that she would, and she did not, we waited in vain. It was quite light on the table, the phantom would have exposed itself all too defencelessly to our view, and to do that did not in the least correspond to the image I had made to myself of the shy, sly, stealthy, equivocal character of our elusive guest: a character too insignificant to have evil intent, on the contrary probably quite well-meaning, but weak-minded and embarrassed. — Nothing further happened. General fatigue, it seemed, had supervened. Willy whispered: " Merry Christmas! " The sitting was over.

It was odd to see in the bald white light the felt ring lying there at my feet where it had no business to be. Remarkable, too, to observe the typed writing on the machine, a perfectly nonsensical jumble of large and small letters; presumably it would have been different if Willy himself knew how to type. He still lay drunk with sleep, leaning sideways across the arm of one of the controls. I went up to him, tapped him on the shoulder, and told him it had been a brilliant sitting. He looked dumbly up at me with his sleepy eyes, and a good-natured, rather sad little smile was on his face.

We moved back by groups into the library, in animated

discussion over what we had seen. Tea was served, and did us all much good. The evening finished off with stage stories narrated by Reicher.

Well, now, what had I seen? Two-thirds of my readers will answer: swindle, sleight-of-hand, deception. Some day, when our knowledge of these matters has progressed, the field will be popularized, and they will deny that such was their judgment. Even now, and even if they take me for a credulous and suggestible fad-chaser, the testimony of trained experimenters like the French scholar Gustave Geley ought to make them less glib. Geley closes his report with the categorical statement: " I do not merely say that there was no deception present in these sittings; I say that the possibility of deception was ruled out." That is absolutely my own position. I am in that intriguing and confounded state of mind in which reason commands us to recognize what reason on the other hand would reject as impossible. The nature of the phenomena I have described makes it inevitable that the idea of deception should afterwards haunt the minds even of those who saw with their own eyes; only to be laid, over and over, by the evidence of the senses, by the reflection that deception was definitely impossible.

But, it will be objected, three-quarters of all the mediums *are* swindlers, and have been exposed as such. — That is a fact, a bewildering one; the more so that in many of these cases, I might even say in most of them, the *dolus*, the intent to deceive, is absent. I am convinced that even our

254

good Willy, if he had had the chance, would have started hocus-pocussing and so have seriously compromised his position; for it is conceivable that in his dream he makes no distinction between what he does with his own hand and what in " other " ways; and being moved by the quite comprehensible desire to produce an effect, he might, if he had been " uncontrolled," have set to, been discovered, and so discredited the experiments. And this would not have been any evidence whatever against the genuineness of the occult phenomena which were produced when he was in safe arrest.

The whole affair, however trifling it looks on the surface, is serious enough to warrant explanations in a serious and even a solemn key. Having seen what I saw, I consider it my duty to bear witness that in the experiments during which I was present, any mechanical deception or sleight-of-hand tricks were humanly impossible. Some may find such testimony reckless; and our reason even obliges and forces us to do so; for we do immediately twist and turn to find a middle way out, by which we may somehow, even verbally, avoid the alternative of deception or reality. " Delusion " is such a word; its very vagueness helps by preventing us from seeing to the bottom of it. The two conceptions of reality and of deception are mingled in it, and perhaps the mingling has more justification than we know, and is less strange in nature than it is to our downright processes of thought. I will say, then, that what I saw had to do with an occult delusion in the domain of organic life; with bewilderingly deep and sub-human complexes, at once

255

primitive and involved. These, undignified by nature and trivial in their activity as they are, are well calculated to be offensive to our proud æsthetic sense, but to deny their abnormal reality would be nothing less than unreasonable obstinacy.

Furthermore, the scientific investigation of these phenomena is no longer precisely in its infancy. Science has at least got so far as to have invented a terminology, by means of which one can express oneself respectably on the subject. What I saw were "telekinetic" phenomena, phenomena of motion at a distance. This particular medium, young Willy S., is especially strong in the production of this kind of manifestations, which in their origins are closely related with the occult natural phenomenon of materialization — in other words, the temporary organization of energy outside the medial organism, its *exteriorization,* so to speak. Among reasonable people it is agreed that the agent which performs the tricks I have described, the swinging of the bell, the lifting of the handkerchief, the typing, is not a spiritistic "intelligence" by the name of Minna, neither is it Aristotle or Napoleon, but the partly exteriorized medium himself. But even that does not go far toward making our problem more accessible to the reason. On the contrary, the popular, spiritualistic hypothesis is much clearer and simpler than the scientific one; while as for the problem of exteriorization and materialization, the longer one looks at it, the more it reveals a complexity apparently calculated for the express purpose of making a mock of the human intellect. Which is not surprising — considering

256

that after all it is bound up with the presumably not occult problem of life itself!

"That which governs life," Claude Bernard wrote, " is neither chemistry nor physics, nor anything of the kind; but the ideal principle of the life-process." A strangely indefinite saying for a great scientist, he being a Frenchman to boot; a saying that gropes vaguely after a mystery, and shows that it is precisely the great world of scholarship which never loses an inward feeling for the mystery; and that only the rank and file run the danger of scientific darkness, unmindful how very little complete, how much mingled with mystery — and riddles perhaps never-to-be-solved — is all their exact knowledge of nature and life and its functions. It is accepted as an established fact in the world of occultism today that the effective and formative principle at work in the psychological processes does in certain cases assume a " teleplastic " character: in other words, it passes beyond the limits of the organism and operates outside it, " ectoplastically." That is, it calls into temporary existence, out of the exteriorized, organic basic substance (the appearance and form of which have already been observed with some degree of exactitude), shapes, limbs, bodily organs, particularly hands, which possess all the properties and functions of normal, physiological, biologically living organs. These teleplastic end-organs move apparently free in space, but so far as can be observed have a close physiological and psychological relation with the medium, in such a way that any impression received through the teleplasm has its effect upon the medial

257

organism, and vice versa. Here we see supra-normal physiology vying with the normal to bear witness to the unity of the organic substance. A fluid, in varying degrees of density, leaves the body of the medium as an amorphous, unorganized mass; takes form in various teleplastic organs, hands, feet, heads, and so on; and after a brief existence in this form, during which, however, it displays all the attributes of living substance, dissolves and is reabsorbed into the medial organism. And this fluid, this substance, this substratum of the various organic formations, is uniform, undifferentiated: there is not such a thing as a bone-substance as different from a muscular or visceral or nervous one; there is only the one substance, the basis and substratum of organic life.

Probably all reasoned thinking and talking in this highly speculative field of facts is today premature and can only seem to clarify without doing so. But one thing is certain: we shall be thinking and talking most inadequately about the phenomena of materialization, as about the riddle of life in general, if we regard them from the physical and material side alone, and not from the psychical as well. It was Hegel who said that the idea, the spirit, is the ultimate source of all phenomena; and perhaps supra-normal physiology is more apt than normal to demonstrate his statement. Yes, it undertakes to place the philosophic demonstration of the primacy of the idea, of the ideal origin of all reality, alongside the biological demonstration of the unity of all organic life.

Quite uninstructed, and on my own responsibility, I explained the telekinetic phenomena as the medium's magically objectivated dreams. And the literature of the subject confirms my explanation; with an awe-inspiring display of technical terms, it explains that the *idea* of the phenomenon, present in the subconsciousness of the somnambulist, mingled moreover with that of the other persons present, is by the aid of psychophysical energy " ectoplastically " moved, by a biopsychical projection, to a certain distance, and imprinted — that is to say, " objectivated." In other words, we call to aid an uninvestigated *ideoplastic* faculty possessed by the medial constitution. Ideoplastic — a word, and a conception, of Platonic power and charm, not without flattering unction to the artist's ear, who will be ready from now on to characterize, not only his own work, but universal reality as ideoplastic phenomena. Yet a word, and a conception, of quite as turbid depths as the word " delusion " itself, and, by virtue of its maddening mixture of elements of the real and the dream, leading straight to the morbid and the preposterous.

Let me give in closing one single but striking example. We are repeatedly assured that the ideoplastic formations, for the time during which they are present, possess all the characteristics of actual life. When they have been in a good mood they have not only let themselves be seen and touched, and their objective reality established by photography and apparatus which registered their telekinetic activities; but plaster casts have been made, hands of transcendental origin having been persuaded to dip themselves into basins of warm water with melted wax floating on top.

In this way a mould has been formed about the spirit member, and hardened by exposure to air. Out of such a mould no human hand could get free without breaking the mould. But the teleplastic organ frees itself by dematerialization, and the experimenters pour plaster of Paris into the wax glove and thus obtain a cast of the materialized organ, which should correspond to it in all particulars. It is to be noted that the casts thus obtained show no resemblance in shape or lines to the hands of the medium, or to those of anyone else present. Now at one of Willy's sittings the following perfectly lunatic thing occurred (and not the only one of its kind). The medium being under the most careful control, a shape like a hand appeared, coming from above and behind, and showed itself above a piece of grey clay on the little table. It had a forearm, and was lighted by a rosy light, and it hovered about over the surface of the clay; on which, after the sitting, six flat impressions were found, on the previously smooth surface. But at the base of Willy's little finger on his left hand, and on the back of the fourth finger of the same hand, *there were traces of clay*.

Now I ask of nature and spirit, I inquire of reason and of logic on her throne: How, when, and from where came the clay on Willy's fingers?

No, I will not go to Herr von Schrenck-Notzing's again. It leads to nothing, or at least to nothing good. I love that which I called the moral upper world, I love the human fable, and clear and humane thought. I abhor luxations of the brain, I abhor morasses of the spirit. Up to now, indeed, I have seen but a few stray sparks from the infernal fires — but that must suffice me. I should like of course to hold, as others have held, a hand like that, a metaphysical delusion made of flesh and blood, in mine. And perhaps there might appear to me, as it has to others, Minna's head, above the shoulder of the sleeping Willy: the head of a charming girl, Slavic in type, with lively black eyes. That, however uncanny, must be a wonderful experience. . . . After all, I will have another try or so with Herr von Schrenck-Notzing; two or three times, not more. That much could do me no harm; and I know myself, I am a man of ephemeral passions; I shall take care that it leads to nothing, and put the whole thing out of my mind for ever after. No, I will not go two or three times, I will only go once, just once more and then not again. I only want to see the handkerchief rise up into the red light before my eyes. For the sight has got into my blood somehow, I cannot forget it. I should like once more to crane my neck, and with the nerves of my digestive apparatus all on edge with the fantasticality of it, once more, just once, see the impossible come to pass.

1923

Thomas Mann is one of the really great contemporary men of letters. He, himself, however roundly resents being labeled a " writer," and insists upon considering himself not as an " artist " at all but only " a good bourgeois drifted by chance into literature." To Mann this is no mere equivocation in terms; rather it represents the very keynote of his philosophy as revealed in his works, springing from a deeply held conviction that the intellectual type is not the ideal toward which evolution moves, but, instead, the man-of-action. All of Mann's writing indeed, from the epoch-making " Buddenbrooks " of his youth to " The Magic Mountain," the masterpiece of his maturity, constitutes the most elaborate rejection in literature of the " intellectual " as an unhealthy growth upon the main body of humanity; but while this theme dominates Mann's works, it is only the scarlet thread in his design, the whole of which comprises nothing less than the most profound criticism of the modern world yet vouchsafed by any novelist.

This book was set on the linotype in Bodoni, electrotyped, printed and bound by The Plimpton Press, Norwood, Mass. The paper was made by S. D. Warren Co., Boston